ACKNOWLEDGE

I would like to acknowledge Suzanne Paizis, deceased July 10, 2004, author of *The Joaquin Castro Adobe in the Twentieth Century---From Earthquake to Earthquake*, for help provided in writing this current book. I met Suzanne a number of years ago when she was searching information for her book. Her research was quite extensive, including personal interviews from past owners and tenants of the Castro Adobe. Because my family owned the Castro Adobe and the house just a short distance from the adobe structure from 1943-45, and we lived in the house, I was selected by Suzanne as a candidate for an interview for her book. After the interview, I provided a section for her book of some of my memories as a lad living on the grounds of the old Rancho San Andrés Castro Adobe, and surrounding area. Subsequently, Suzanne and I became friends. She along the way encouraged me to continue writing about the Castro Adobe, and cordially offered access to her research and pictorial collection.

Edna Kimbro, whom I got to know during her days of fighting for the restoration of the Castro Adobe, had a strong impact on my current writing. She was such a great influence upon everyone who was concerned about the fate of the Castro Adobe. It is no wonder that after her death August 6, 2003, two hundred friends and colleagues from around the world gathered at the Santa Cruz Historic Park to share their respect and love for her.

The Pajaro Valley Historical Association is to be commended both for research and a number of photographs that were used in this book. They have done a wonderful job in keeping the population of the Pajaro Valley informed of the history of the valley.

Through effective leadership by the Friends of Santa Cruz State Parks, its directors and hard working staff, Friends has grown to be the second largest of 84 similar non-profit partners in California. It has done a great job contributing to the restoration of the Castro Adobe, and all members are to be commended. Contributions from their wonderful blog have added greatly to research of this book and I graciously thank them.

PREFACE

The purpose of this book is to present an historical account of special events associated with the unique hacienda known as the Rancho San Andrés Castro Adobe, near Watsonville, California, along with a chronology of owners and stories throughout its era. It sets high on a ridge off a narrow country road in Larkin Valley, today being one of Santa Cruz County's historic gems.

When I was a young lad my family bought about 40 acres, including both the Castro Adobe and the old house near the adobe structure, one which we moved into in October, 1943. Understandably, some of the memories and events noted here during my short era of living there will be those of mine and my immediate family, and will consequently be included along with many others generated throughout time. However, ours represent only a small portion of the total conglomerate of the main body of history and will not particularly be over emphasized. On the other hand, a first hand view is often more valid than a hand me down one; so that is why some of my family history will be included and added to the over-all historical contribution, and perhaps be helpful.

The span of time from 1833, when Jose Joaquin Castro received title to the Rancho, until the year 2009, when the Castro Adobe was recently totally renovated and earthquake proofed, covers many years and much has happened during this long interval. But the Castro Adobe's survival to live has brought about change. It has existed as a living house throughout its many years, in spite of periods of vacancy and neglect, because each family that lived there changed it and made repairs, as they felt necessary. It would be dreadful to imagine what would have become of the Castro Adobe had it not been structurally cared for by all the private owners in this last century. Without such efforts, perhaps there would only be mounds of mud up on a hill, shards, and maybe a few pieces of rusted metal. Without author Suzanne Paizis' patient and thorough research, many vital parts of the Castro Adobe history would be missing. She spent years and traveled many miles to contact representatives of every family who occupied the adobe. She conducted personal interviews and searched public libraries and archives for legal documents, newspaper articles, and other references. Her research resulted in a century-long and well documented update of chronicles during this evolution. We owe much to Suzanne Paizis and also to Edna Kimbro, both who once lived in the Castro Adobe.

INTRODUCTION

Suzanne Paizis' book, *Joaquin Castro Adobe in the Twentieth Century---From Earthquake to Earthquake,* initiated an incentive with me to promote further historical writing about the of the Castro Adobe, some of which is brought out in my book entitled, *The Rancho San Andrés Castro Adobe.* It is hoped this book can serve as a complement to Suzanne's informative book. It was written with encouragement and help from her.

Because research both by Suzanne Paizis and me is similar in content in some cases, some of our descriptions may appear to be somewhat overlapped, and in some cases similar, due principally because they were often sought from the same sources. Therefore, it is pertinent to present this introduction in a manner which coincides with both researches. This is done partly in lieu of Suzanne's previous offer of excerpts and pictures from her book for my writings. Deeming them useful and helpful, I felt honored and fortunate to incorporate some of them. Subsequently, sections of her research and mine may be intermingled elsewhere in my book, resulting in a conglomerate of valid research from both parties, as might be detected in the continuation of this introduction and elsewhere.

While men on the eastern coast of the future United States of America were busy putting together a democratic government, a little boy of seven trudged from Mexico to northern California with his parents and the Anza party. Spain was still far from Madrid, or even from Sinaloa, Mexico, where he was born. They came as volunteer soldiers/settlers and brought their wives, children, horses and cattle with them to the new settlement. It was this willingness to begin life in an unknown land that was later rewarded by the Mexican government when many of these settlers' sons were granted the great Ranchos of California.

Juan Bautista de Anza (1735-1788), Spanish explorer and official, was the leader of the group. Some time before 1769, and during the establishment of the Alta California missions, the Spanish government recognized the importance of securing California from outside intervention, and in 1770 the seat of government was changed from Loreto to Baja California to Monterey. The 1775-1776 Anza overland expedition was the first emigration of Spanish settlers specifically recruited to colonize the area. The remarkable thing about Anza's captaincy is that of the 240 people who made the journey, only one did not survive, a woman dying in childbirth, while three new infants were added to the group. Among those on the historic trek were Joaquin Isidro Castro, his wife, and their nine children.

The boy, Jose Joaquin Castro (son of Joaquin Isidro Castro and future grantee of Rancho San Andrés) arrived in the Monterey Bay area in 1776. Twenty-two years later, he settled at the Villa de Branciforte, a new pueblo on the bluff overlooking what is now the city of Santa Cruz, California. Most likely Jose Joaquin participated in the horse races reported to have been held on this very same street around two hundred years ago. The Villa de Branciforte was one of three pueblos established in Alta California, the others being in Los Angeles and San Jose. Located on the east side of present day Santa Cruz, above the San Lorenzo River and less than two miles from the Santa Cruz Mission, the site was established in 1797. Again, recruitment was the method of populating an area, and Jose Joaquin Castro, who had been a soldier at the Monterey Presidio for a decade, came with his wife and children to take up residency at Branciforte at that time.

Over the next quarter century, putting together a new city was difficult: relations with the mission padres were not always friendly, government authorities were distant and having their own problems. At the end of the revolution in 1821, Mexico gained independence from Spain. The local residents were no longer part of the Spanish empire, and those of the first generation thought of themselves as *Californios*. Although government officials did not consider Villa de Branciforte a success, it was doing well enough to survive as the vast Ranchos were granted to the great "Dons" of the period. Today it is part of the city of Santa Cruz.

By 1823 Jose Joaquin Castro was granted a provisional concession from Mexico to the Rancho San Andrés, a respectable spread of two square leagues (a league is approximately 4400 acres), ranging from Monterey Bay to Corralitos, and from the Pajaro River to Aptos. Along with his sons and daughters, their family holdings eventually included the greater part of what is now Santa Cruz County, from Pajaro to Aptos to Soquel, and almost to Davenport, consisting of over 250,000 acres.

In the early 1800s Castro family members were among California's first settlers, their "wealth" being in immense land holdings and cattle, their prominence great. Jose Joaquin Castro had married Antonia Amador in 1791, and with her had fifteen children, though not all survived. After Antonia's death in 1827, he married young Maria del Rosario Briones. Legend has it that he built the big adobe for the young bride. Romantic as that seems today, exactly when construction was first started or when completed is still a murkey question, although some historians have attempted to ascribe specific dates for the occasion. Jose Joaquin Castro received title to the Rancho in 1833. He and Maria produced three or four more children. His household grew to accommodate his offspring as well as the families of his older children.

By the time Don Jose Joaquin Castro died in 1838, the lifestyle of the rancheros was coming to an end. In 1822 Mexico had replaced Spain as the government, and only a few more years were to pass before American rule supplanted Mexican. Land hungry men were swarming into California, either crossing mountains and deserts or disembarking from ships up and down the coast. The immense holdings of the Dons on their Ranchos would not survive this invasion. Now each newcomer wanted his own parcel of this magnificent countryside. A few married into local *Californio* families, while others found ways to get what they sought with help from the many American lawyers who came west to assist in the task. Jose Joaquin's son Juan Jose and other family members continued to live in or around the big house on the hill. By 1870, however, the legal disputes, the avaricious Yankees, and a severe drought signaled an end to the vast holdings and dominance of the family. Just how and when the Castros lost their lands and their fine house is a story for another teller.

Seven adobes were found in the Pajaro Valley in 1850, among them those of the Castro, Amesti, Rodriguez, and Vallejo families. All are now gone, with the exception of the Castro Adobe. The house has great historical significance, as it is the only surviving rancho hacienda of the Mexican Colonial period. To view the other adobes, one has to search files for photographs. Even the mounds and stone foundations, which remained for awhile, have vanished. The San Andreas fault lies just a few miles from the Rancho San Andrés Castro Adobe. Two major earthquakes, one in 1906, the other in 1989 have occurred. Both had a dramatic impact on the Rancho San Andrés Castro Adobe, which still stands as the grandest of all adobe buildings representing Northern California's rancho period. This hacienda features a spacious *fandango* room on the second floor and an original one-story *cocina*, one of only five such Mexican kitchens remaining in the state. With its long, two-story proportions and full-width balcony, it is a distinctly Monterey-Colonial building that demonstrates the expansion to the countryside of this celebrated architectural form from its original urban setting, at the end of the Mexican era (1821-1848)

In 1988, adobe conservationist Edna Kimbro, and her husband, Joe, purchased the Castro Adobe from 20-year stewards, David and Elizabeth Potter. It was during the Kimbro's tenure that the 1969 Loma Prieta Earthquake severely damaged the house, but it was also during the Kimbro years when huge steps were taken to preserve the adobe for future generations. The restoration of the

Castro Adobe will be the fulfillment of Edna's and others' tireless efforts, personally and professionally, to bring the building to its former glory.

A Castro relative is pictured here with Margaret Holtzclaw during the ceremony in 2002 when the the Castro Asobe was acquired by California State Parks. There were numerous Castro relatives at this ceremony as well as ex-owners and friends of the Castro Adobe.

The 1906 San Francisco earthquake brought an end to the adobe as their home when the worried Hansens built another house to live in. Again as the century was coming to a close, another severe earthquake drove residents Joseph and Edna Kimbro and their sons from the shaking structure. Once more the marvelous house was uninhabited, "condemned," falling into disrepair, encircled by wire fencing and yellow tape warning signs. Over the last decade, owner Edna Kimbro's focus was to save the historic structure even though she would never live in it again. Little did she know that October 17, 1989, was the last time a family would ever breakfast in that kitchen. Her account of the destruction later that day brought to a close another chapter of a family and another century of the adobe as it was lived in and loved.

Recently, ex-owners, their families, Castro relations, and others associated with the Castro Adobe in the past came together during the dedication of the adobe to be made a State Park. My wife, Margaret, and I were happy to attend this historical event and to meet so many people associated with the the Castro Adobe in the past. One by one this group of people came together to be part of the history of the Castro Adobe.

One time back in Castro history, such a gathered group would be watching for the cloud of rising dust from rival Amesti family horses heading for the Pajaro River where the Castro sentinels could quickly spur their steeds to head them off and charge a fee for crossing. Instead, a group gathered at this time sees the blinking red signals of planes taking off and landing at the Watsonville Airport, and can follow moving freeway lights as cars crisscross former Castro lands. Now as the 21st century unfolds, we know the Castro Adobe will continue to survive up on the hill. This historically precious, beloved house will soon be available for all to enjoy--a brief moment when a visitor is able to return in spirit to the time when the Castro Adobe was first built and all the land viewed from that vantage point was owned by the Casrtos.

Acquired by California State Parks in 2002, the Rancho San Andrés Castro Adobe currently sits on one acre of land that contains a small orchard. An important and unusual aspect of the adobe is its rural location that retains much of the cultural landscape of the rancho era, and the original *Carreta Path*--Old Adobe Road. The authentic early-California building and its setting possess tremendous potential for interpretation of the rural lifestyle and culture of Mexican California for the benefit of present-day residents of Pajaro Valley, Santa Cruz County, and Central Coast region. The Rancho San Andrés Castro Adobe will now realize its ultimate potential, having been stabilized and restored, recently completed in 2009.

CONTENTS

Acknowledgements 1

Preface 2

Introduction 3

Contents 7

One	Early owners of the Castro Adobe	9
Two	The Alvin Holtzclaw Era	17
Three	The George Holtzclaw Era	26
Four	William and Maude Nelson Years	47
Five	John and Suzanne Pazis Occupancy	55
Six	The Victor and Sidney Family Come to the Adobe	63
Seven	David and Elizabeth Potter Buy the Castro Adobe	69
Eight	Joseph and Edna Kimbro's Short Stay at the Castro Adobe	74
Nine	Friends of Santa Cruz State Parks Begin Their Work	91
Ten	An Early Outlook	113
Eleven	Beginning to Present	120..
Twelve	Castro Families	124..
Thirteen	Joaquin and bandit Vasquez	.138
Fourteen	Summary	149

ONE

The purpose in writing this book is to preserve historical events related to Rancho San Andrés Castro Adobe, make the reader aware of the chronology of past owners of the property, and to learn of persons instrumental in the structure's fate in it remaining a stable entity. Following the early Castro era, the non-hispanic era began in 1883.

On October 29, 1883, Hans Hansen received the title to the Rancho San Andrés Castro Adobe with thirty-nine acres of Larkin Valley land several miles north of Watsonville, California, within the Monterey Bay area. The Castro Adobe sets high on a ridge and off a narrow country lane passing through Larkin Valley. The Castro Adobe was built in the mid-1800s by Jose Joaquin Castro and son Juan Jose, and has added a rich history to the fertile Pajaro Valley. The Hansens were the first owners of the Castro Adobe since the Castro family. It is believed that when the Hansens moved into the adobe the Castros were still in residence there. If true, it is possible Hans Hansen rented the property until the time he

The earliest known picture of the Joaquin Castro Adobe, about 1890. Note the large barn and team of horses hitched to a carriage at far right and Hansen family in front of the Castro Adobe. Courtesy of E. Lee Hansen Collection.

purchased it. Regardless, Hansen was living in Rancho San Andrés in 1875, so he was in the general area earlier than the year he took legal title to the Castro Adobe in 1883. Later, in 1897, when Hans resided with his family on the land and premises, his family consisted of a wife and five minor children, at which time the estimated cash value of the property was $4,000.

The first earliest known photo of the Castro Adobe, shown above, was made possibly about 1889-90. Accordingly to Edna Kimbro, this is the only picture of any historic adobe that demonstrates lumbering and is very significant. "Lumbering" is a Spanish way of covering over the gable end of a building in order to provide space for storage or housing of animals, as well as to protect the weather end. In the case of adobe construction, it is also protection of the somewhat fragile clay material. It can be noticed in this photo that the adobe bricks under the wooden gable above the lumbering boards are exposed, not plastered over, painted, or whitewashed. The steep staircase at the left of the building is seen rising to the second floor verandah; it was later revised to a much less steeper incline. At the far right of the building can be noted the old barn that was torn down during a later era. Someone riding in a buggy and steering a two-team of horses is vaguely pictured at the extreme right of the adobe.

Hans is shown near the center of the picture, bearded and wearing a hat. The seated woman to his left is Han's wife Margaretta, holding Hannah on her lap. The little boy standing near the stairs is Andrew. The two elder children are H.C. (Chris) up on the veranda and Guarde to the right of her mother below. Nissen, the youngest known, may not have been born yet.

The picture below shows the Hansen family gathered in front of the Castro Adobe and on the veranda. Of note is that the stair case going up to the veranda as seen in earlier pictures is missing; albeit, the imprint of the old staircase is seen on the wall. It is evident though that there is access to the upper story elsewhere at this time, as Margaretta is seen on the veranda holding Hannah, with Gertrude on the left. This is substantiated because it has been noted that Hans made things more convenient for the family when he built an inside staircase; although when the outside one was removed is still in question.

On the ground floor yard is Hans wearing a hat and vest, with two walking sticks or crutches. The boy with the dog at far right is probably Andrew, who is about four years older than Hanna behind the fence, at Hans' left. It can be noted that previous lumbering has been removed on the south wall and new plaster and whitewash cover the previous bare bricks.

After 43 years the Hansens were no longer at the adobe. The 1906 San Francisco earthquake had damaged the Castro Adobe structure and because of that, the new house that Hans built became their residence. Local lore tells us that the Hansens moved into the other house shortly after the earthquake; assuming

A later view of the Hansen family in front of the Castro Adobe.

perhaps that by this time Hans had already built the house that they moved into; the exact date of its construction is unknown, for there were no building permits or other fees to pinpoint its date.

Suzanne Paizis gives an excellent description of some of the damage that was caused by the San Francisco earthquake in that area in her book, *The Joaquine Castro Adobe in the Twentieth Century,* and follows below:

> Early April mornings at the Castro Adobe are always a bit nippy, and frequently a low fog dampens everything as dawn comes to the Larkin Valley At 5:00 a.m. on the morning in 1906 the master and mistress of the house, Hans and Margaretta Hansen, may still have been abed, pushing back the minutes until they would have to rise and start to begin the daily chores around the Rancho.
>
> 'The eighteenth of April, 1906, at 5:13 in the morning, one of the most severe earthquakes ever recorded since the beginning of the civilized habitation visited the State of California. Very important destruction to engineering works occurred in a belt about fifty miles wide and nearly three hundred miles in length, extending along the Pacific Coast, with the

Bay of San Francisco at its center', so wrote Charles Derleth, Jr., publishing it on April 18, 1907, one year to the day after the disaster. It seems appropriate to have this opinion from a structural engineer who was on the spot back then and who described the San Francisco disaster in those terms.

Today natural disasters like earthquakes are highly publicized through books, documentaries, movies, and radio and television programs. The science of plate tectonics is a favorite high school essay topic. In the 20th century earthquakes have destroyed cities all over the world and killed thousands of people in numbers and terms that even a sophisticated structural engineer of 1906 could not have imagined. Still, on that April morning, the San Francisco earthquake dramatically changed the lives of most of the people along the California coast. Hans and Margaretta were among them.

There were aftershocks, enough to keep people on edge. The local reports and incredible news of the destruction from San Francisco must have added to the insecurity for weeks, as was the situation for everyone else in northern California. Because those who have experienced mild quakes while living in the Castro Adobe, they can easily recall the furious shaking of those handmade bricks, and the sudden alarming awareness of the weight of the place. That made it possible to imagine the reactions of people following a quake of the magnitude of the San Francisco event.

The Watsonville *Register Pajaronian* claimed that Ford's department Store moved a distance of 7.3 feet, although later modified that statement. They also reported that the cement floor of the Big Creek Power Company sank in spots to a depth of several feet, with the water tank listing badly, the furnaces unusable. The two big brick chimneys at the high school fell through the tile and metal roof. One located itself in the senior room and one fell into the sophomore room. Chimneys and walls tumbled down all over town while the contents of businesses and houses were in "a wrecked condition of affairs." The bridge across the Pajaro River was thrown out of plumb, with piers ruptured, moved by inches, and now impassable. Dramatic tales of close calls and miraculous luck in avoiding misfortune were frequent. Fleeing refugees from the north nervously passed through the area or found temporary lodging with local relatives and friends. In one house about half the plaster was thrown from every northern and southern wall on the first floor...but not from the upper rooms. "A bureau moved eastward three feet from the wall," states a government report of the fateful day. The old building was not identified. However, if this describes what may have then occurred in the Castro Adobe, one can understand the consternation of the family's actions below:

Frank Mello in front of the *cocina* in about 1939. Note the over-grown veranda and deteriated roof. Couresy of Pajaro Valley Historical Association.

Such was the turmoil of the time, and out of the situation a story emerged that the Hansens were so disturbed by the shaking they quickly built a second house nearby and moved out of the adobe. Conjecture, probability, and likelihood are words that may be used in this context as to when this metal-roofed house went up, and if, and for how long the family lived in it. We will never be certain of the exact circumstances from those angst-ridden days; however, the result, a building which was situated about forty yards from the adobe, still stands, and has been continually inhabited ever since.

The last quarter of the nineteenth century had already brought great changes to the San Andrés Rancho. Beef, hides and tallow were the product of Castro's immense land holdings and herds. Spanish was the language in and around the earthen building where many family members and friends gathered in the *cocina (kitchen)* and under the c*orredor* (verandah). Further changes occurred when the Hansens came, as English replaced Spanish and the vast herds disappeared when the number of acres was reduced from thousands to only thirty-nine.

The south end and back of the adobe building, showing a sagging roof, deterioation and plaster fallen from the walls. Of note is the raised roof pitch that was done in the 1890s when Hans Hansen re-roofed it. It looked this way a number of years before the Holtzclaw family owned the property, but later was lowered to original pitch. Courtesy of Pajaro Valley Hiistorical Association.

It seems that from the time the Hansen's lived in the Hansen house, it has always been occupied. The Hansen, Schueller, Waite, Maderos, Mello Sr., Mello Jr., and Alvin Holtzclaw families, owners between 1906 when it was possibly built, and 1945 when it was made into separate parcels, most lived in it at one time or another. New owners of the Castro Adobe property often used this second house as their main residence, while the adobe was often vacant and looked upon as a curious old barn where teenagers carved their initials on the walls. But for the string of the adobe property owners up to 1945, the newer building with the galvanized metal roof was usually home.

North view of the *cocina* attached to the Castro Adobe. Note the horse drawn buggy at corner of cocina. Courtesy of Pajaro Valley Historical Association.

There was quite an extensive chronology of ownership of the Castro Adobe and Hansen house ownership throughout the years since the Castro era. Following is a chronology of ownership up through 1945; Other owners will be discussed more extensively farther within the book:

On October 29, 1883, Hans and Margaretta Hansen received title to the Joaquin Castro Adobe with 39 acres of Larkin Valley land from the San Francisco attorney A. B .Patrick for $15,000, retaining title (1883-1914); On April 22, 1914, Casper I. and Minnie J. Schueller gained title to the Hansen house and Castro Adobe, and thirty-nine acres, (1914-1915); Ada and J.C. Westphall received title on March 24, 1915, from C.I. Schueller that included the Castro Adobe, the Hansen house, and 39 acres, (1915-1917); On October 31, 1917, Meda L. Waite received title from Ada Westphal that included the Castro Adobe, Hansen house, and 39 acres. The Waites were orchardists and grew apricots, pears and apples and used the adobe structure for drying the fruit and for storage. During these years it was also used for storage, (1917-1924); Meda L. Waite sold the Castro Adobe, Hansen house and property to Manuel E. and Mary R. Maderos in 1924. When Manuel and Mary bought the property, they too moved into the second house and lived there for a decade until Manuel's death on the premises on June 22, 1935. Manuel never lived in the adobe, while Mary resided in both houses, (1924-1935); On September 16, 1935, Frank and Mary Mello received title from the First National Bank of San Jose that included the Castro Adobe, Hansen house and 39 acres. The estimated value of the property was $4,000. They did much restoration work there, continued to live in the restored adobe until his death on January 17, 1943. Soon after she moved out and would not return again as mistress of the historic place, (1935-1940); On June 20, 1940, Frank Jr. and Vivian Mello received the title from his father Frank Mello, Sr., that included the Castro Adobe, the Hansen house and 39 acres.

Research shows that about the time Frank Jr. took possession of the property he moved into the Hansen house while his father continued to live in the Castro Adobe with his second wife, Mary Maderos Mello. He assumed an indebtedness of $4,530, (1940-1943); Six months after Frank's death, Frank Jr. Mello sold the Castro Adobe and property to Alvin R. and Esther J. Holtzclaw, (1943-1945). When the family first moved into the house next to the Castro Adobe, the large two-story structure was vacant and unused.; it also was actually in a rather degraded condition.

TWO

It was in October of 1943 Alvin Holtzclaw realized he could not effectively grow avocados on his ten acre ranch just a few miles south of Watsonville. To grow avocados was his dream, but now it was questionable to grow them there. When he bought the place he did not realize that it sometimes got very cold in the winter—unsuitable for avocados. As time passed, he became more convinced that avocados could not grow at this low elevation, where heavy frosts may in the winter months occur. His family had been living in this area, a suburb of Watsonville called Elkhorn, for only about two years. Several of the neighbors had become Alvin's good friends and discouraged him against his proposed avocado venture. One of them told him he would be crazy to plant avocados there; a higher elevation, where frosts were not so extreme would be required. Al mauled this over, and soon afterwards he announced to the family that they would soon be moving.

Al immediately began to look around the Watsonville outskirts to find a place with a higher elevation. He located a 39 acre plot a few miles north of Watsonville, in a pretty green valley called Larkin Valley. The property he found was high on the ridge of the valley's eastern side. He knew he had found the ideal spot. It should be relatively frost-free in this area, as he was told by local residents. After seeing the property, he came home and was very exuberant about a possible move to Larkin Valley. He announced to the family that they would have to visit Larkin Valley the next week-end and see this nice place he found. If they liked it as much as he, then they should buy it. He felt this would be an ideal area, not only to grow avocados, but also to rear his children.

The next week-end he took the family out to this property he liked so well, and it immediately appealed to everyone. The property was situated high above the valley's floor, and elevated enough to be free from heavy frosts. Upon observation of the property, the family noted several intriguing structures were contained on the grounds; a house with a sheet-metal roof, a large water tank on a stand, a big barn which looked exciting to the children, and a huge two-story adobe building, even more exciting. It all appeared to all the kids as a place of adventure! Esther, their mother, liked the place as well, because it was near a school. The family was large now, containing nine children. All, except one, were in school. Larkin Valley Elementary School was only a short walk from the house, so the location was ideal in this respect. The ranch also had a grove of apricot trees which all admired; everyone agreed, and the property was bought for the sum of five thousand and-seven hundred dollars, a price considered nominal at this time.

The view of the Castro Adobe as viewed from the Holtzclaw residence at the Hansen house. Note the water tank and tower seen at left during tthis time. Courtesy of Sallie Millang Collection.

The family moved into the house located only a short distance from the large adobe structure. Later they learned their house to be called the Hansen house, a name derived from a distant owner; along with the Castro Adobe, both had interesting histories. The Hansen house was an old, wooden-frame structure with the original corrugated metal roofing; albeit, somewhat rusty. It is said to have been built in 1906. It had foot wide vertical cedar siding, their joining edges being lapped with narrower strips. The house contained five bedrooms, living room, kitchen, bath, back porch, and pantry. On a nearby wall in the kitchen hung an antique telephone, but not considered so at that time. The family can recall being on a two party line. When the phone rang twice it was for them and when thrice, for the Thompson family on the apple farm at the end of Old Adobe Road. To reach the operator simply required turning the handle on the side of the phone a few turns.

The front porch of the house faced out onto Old Adobe Road, from there a drive passed the Hansen house, turned up past the old water-tank tower near the

Castro Adobe and then swung down past the front of the Castro Adobe to again joined Old Adobe Road. The Holtzclaws and the Thompsons comprised the only residences along Old Adobe Road, the latter being located at the far end of the road. To the right of the family's front porch was a large Bartlett pear tree, one

Alvin Holtzclaw with a first avacado tree planted in his orchard. Note the existing mature apricot trees in the background. Courtesy of the Holtzclaw Collection.

This is a picture of the Castro Adobe as it appered when the two oldest boys of the Holtzclaw family, Rodney and Kenneth, moved into the bottom floor for awhile, during renovation of the Hansen house. Courtesy of the Holtzclaw Collection.

that spread over onto the porch area. Many vividly recall picking delicious, ripe pears from the porch, and still remember how great they tasted.

The family seldom used this front entrance, however, for it was much more convenient to use the side entrance of the house, one leading directly into a room used as the living room. At one time the large room directly in front of the house facing Old Adobe Road served as the living room. It now served the family as the master bedroom. The room that they now used for the living room was perhaps once a family room, or parlor. Some can vividly recall the amazement of the younger kids when they first stepped into the large living room, exclaiming what a large room it was.

The back porch was bordered by a small grove of apricot trees, numbering around forty trees. Nearby was a smoke house. Once in awhile one of the kids would peek into this little structure, for they were always curious. Two of the younger ones once stuck their heads into the smoke house and quickly pulled back. They did not like the terrible smell in there. Actually, it was the odor of burnt sulfur, for the smoke house was equipped with a container for burning sulfur at its bottom, and trays for holding the dried halved apricots, stacked above. This was a procedure required for keeping the dried fruit a colorful orange, allowing it not to oxidize to a displeasing brown, tasteless, dark color.

Some of the family spent many hours tending this orchard, as it required pruning, spraying, and yes, picking the fruit. This work was left to next oldest child, Ken, and his father, as the younger brothers were too young to help and older brother Rodney was soon off to the army. Next to the apricot trees was a fertile plot of soil which was later used to grow corn.

It was at this time Ken, got a job working for Mr. Thompson involving feeding his hogs and doing odd jobs around his apple ranch, and oh yes, picking apples. Eventually, he gave him an old mule that he no longer needed and considered worthless; its name was Jude. He said he no longer needed it because he purchased a new tractor. He said the mule was a good worker. Ken was so happy and it came complete with harness, reins, and a harrow for tilling the ground. He took a liking to the old mule and subsequently became its guardian; and ultimately was the one found behind the harrow preparing the ground to plant corn. He was fourteen years old at this time, but was perfectly capable of hitching the old mule up, taking it out on the field plot to do the ground preparation.

Everything usually went quite well, but once in awhile old Jude would decide enough was enough, and stop cold, refusing to move or budge at all. However, just when Ken decided to do something else while it stood there motionless, it came to life. There it would go…down the field, harrow and all, and not stop until it was slowed by him running and grabbing the reins and pulling back to stop Jude. He certainly then understood the familiar expression: "Stubborn as a mule."

Ken is pictured behind the harrow which his mule Jude is pulling to prepare the soil for planting a corn crop. Courtesy of the Holtzclaw Collection.

Jude was usually kept out to pasture, but sometimes brought into the small building located next to the apricot orchard. Ken's dad enjoyed getting his avocado trees planted and they adapted quite well. As previously mentioned, across the way from the Hansen house stood the large two-story Castro Adobe, but at this time was totally neglected. It appeared not been lived in for quite awhile; doubtlessly used for storage as evidence seemed to indicate, although there was nothing much inside it.

A short distance from the north end of the Castro Adobe, set back from the structure, was located a large barn. It had a gable roof, containing a lean-to on one side, which had once been used to house farm animals, or perhaps as a dairy barn. The floor of the lean-to was cement; whereas, the barn had dirt for a floor. The main arena of the barn supported evidence of having once been a storage place for hay and farm equipment. Its central roof structure was rather dilapidated, giving the appearance that it could soon fall to the ground. The north-east side of the Castro Adobe faced a pasture land which separated it from Mr. Thompson's apple orchard, where he grew several varieties of apples, such as Newtown Pippin and Bellflower. During this era apples were grown in this area quite extensively.

A picturesque water-tower stood to the right of the adobe structure and only a short distance from its front entrance. The framework supported a large wooden tank atop, one which once served as a water reserve. Below the tank, the area had been converted to a living quarters, but more recently only used for storage, a utilization that the family subscribed for also.

Some of the Holtzclaw children, starting from left: Duane, Gene, Lois, Wanda, Dale, Beverly and Spencer sitting in front. Duane and Gene were the two tree climbers, and Gene was the one who damaged Dad's favorite avocado tree by climbing to its top and bending it to the ground, when it broke at the trunk. Courtesy of the Holtzclaw Collection.

When the family arrived before they could became comfortably settled in their new house, they needed to do some renovation. It was rather large, but several rooms needed attention before they could completely adequately move in. They now took more notice of the Castro Adobe nearby and decided to use one of its rooms while renovating their residence. Therefore, the two oldest boys of the family, Rod and Ken temporarily situated themselves on the bottom floor of the adobe structure, and remained there for some time while renovation was in progress at the Hansen house. They were no doubt the first inhabitants of the building since many years. The first night they attempted to move into this dark, spacious area of the bottom floor they found the front door barred; however, one of the large front windows was missing, and it was easy to just crawl through the

The Alvin and Esther Holtzclaw children at home at the Hansen house. From left: Spencer, Dale, Gene, Lois, Duane, Beverely, and Wanda. Courtesy of the Holtzclaw Collection.

widow sill. At this time they were impressed with the thickness of the adobe wall, for had never seen anything like that before. Soon they came out and unbarred the front door, making entry easier.

Understandably, there was no water, electricity, or other utility piped into the structure. Regardless, being boys, they pretended this adventure to be a camp outing. They set up their bedding near a large pot-belly stove in the room, no doubt at one time used for heating. There was no entrance to the upper floor from the bottom floor within the building. The only access to the upper floor was via a stairway outside. It was cool at night in the large adobe house and they were tempted to drag in some wood and start a fire in the old stove, but this was decided against, fearing the condition of the stove. The old stove vent did not look very secure; in fact part of it appeared to be broken and loose as it passed through a window plate.

Of course, the boys had access to the house where the rest of the family remained; here they would eat their meals. Their quarters in the adobe structure were equipped rather meagerly. Most importantly, perhaps, was a lantern; albeit, one which only partially lighted up the large room on one side of the large pot-belly stove nearby where they were camped. Also a very large wooden table was there, whose longer side faced the stove. It appeared big enough for corporate members of some company to surround and hold their board meetings. They later recalled it was the only furniture to be seen in the room. Here they placed the lantern, and other items of their camping adventure. The floor on this bottom level was constructed with large, thick and wide planking. One evening when they sat around the big table, they could not help but witness the lantern's effulgent gleaming, so vividly pronounced below onto the floor's magnanimous structure.

It was now they remembered a story their father's realtor related to him as the boys sat and listened in awe. However, in retrospect, the narrative was probably primarily directed to them, as the realtor seemed to greatly enjoy arousing their interest. He told of the legend held that a senior member of the Castro family had buried a large amount of gold at this site, subsequently dying, prior to disclosing its whereabouts. The boys surmised---possibly this horde might be just under those thick boards below their feet. They discussed this possibility to some extent, and were elated to a frenzy, at which extreme they were almost ready to begin removing planks.

However, the evening was subsiding, and they were soon under their covers and sound asleep and the gold under the floor was soon forgotten. Regardless, the realtor's story no doubt sustained its desired effect upon them. They often questioned where this treasure might be. It certainly added some inquisitive exploration around the Castro Adobe for quite awhile. However, Al's children were not the only ones excited about a possible treasure of gold that some believed to be somewhere on the property. However, no treasure was ever found that was known about.

THREE

The fate of the old Castro Adobe remained in limbo for a short while after it was sold by Frank Jr. Mello to Alvin Holtzclaw in 1943, standing there unoccupied for only a short while though until it was sold to George Holtzclaw.

When Alvin moved onto the adobe property in 1943 the adobe was essentially vacant, although had previously been used for storage. Soon after the Holtzclaw family moved into the Hansen house near the Castro Adobe, they realized that it was to be soon reoccupied, beginning a string of occupants who were to habitat the building once again.

The reoccupation of the Castro Adobe came around this time due to the activity of Alvin's Uncle George and Aunt Georgia. They on occasion came to visit the family, and soon had taken a liking to the old adobe building. As time passed, their love of the house inflamed and they made Alvin an offer to buy it and a small surrounding acreage. He accepted their offer.

Uncle George's priority before concentrating on renovation of the adobe structure and moving into it was to get a small dairy established on his property. There was a lean-to on the old barn nearby, previously used as a dairy barn, with a cement floor and rooms for stanchions for milking cows. Soon Uncle George purchased ten Holstein milk cows and was in the dairy business. He pastured his cows on the lowland bog below. He hired some of Alvin's older children to help with the milking and feeding, which they were happy to oblige.

During the day the cows grazed in their pasture, but near milking time could be seen approaching through the fenced runway that Uncle George had erected from the bog below to the barn. Every morning and evening Uncle George's cows would come up from the pasture to be milked, passing by the little barn where Bessey, "Wanda's cow" filed off to be milked in her habitat, usually by Wanda. The kids used to like to watch them pass by in single file during milking time. They needed only a call from the ridge above to begin their journey to the barn. The pathway that Uncle George had constructed for his cows to walk from the pasture to his dairy barn, became a show place for the kids to gather and watch them.

The part of the farm life that all the older children enjoyed most, though, was raising calves. Uncle George and Al became partners in this venture. Mr. Siebring, Al's ex-neighbor, kept them supplied with as many newborn calves as they could handle and Uncle George provided milk from his cows to feed them when young. The kids cared for them until they became old enough to sell to a buyer, who would pick them up when sold.

George Holtzclaw soon after moving into the Castro Adobe after he bought it including a parcel of the the property. Courtesy of the Holtzclaw Collection.

They were usually housed in the barn but usually during the day would be put out in the corral beside the barn. It was some fun when the calves got older for the younger ones in the family to ride them around in the corral; occasionally, though, one would get bucked off and land in the soft dirt.

In the subsequent days, weeks, and months that followed, Uncle George made numerous improvements to his purchase. He began the task of remodeling the adobe house's first floor, first starting with creating a living room and kitchen, below. When this phase was finished he and his wife moved into the house and

Uncle George's new car was greatly admired by the Holtzclaw children who were often given rides in it. Buying a new car in Larkin Valley where the Castro Adobe was located was quite rare during this time. Courtesy of the Holtzclaw collection.

slowly worked on other parts of the structure. The kids began to develop a close fellowship with them. They often can recall many pleasant hours sitting around visiting in their comfortable living room, playing Chinese checkers, or other games of that era. They always referred to them as "Uncle George and Aunt Georgia," although George was their great-uncle.

Of course, the upper story of their adobe residence, as is recalled, remained untouched. It retained the open spaciousness that it had always held, serving in the past as a fandango ball room. Everyone enjoyed this room, and the younger kids that were allowed to often play there found it very exciting. They were quite aware of the long metal tie bars that extended from the south end wall, dropping at an angle and anchored to the floor. They used to swing from these bars, but had no idea of there purpose. They had been installed there after the 1906 earthquake, in order to stabilize the vertical south wall that had been slightly disrupted, and also help support stableness of the spacious floor of the fandango room. When the Holtzclaw children played there years ago when the building was uninhabited, they found the floor quite giggly. They still remember the fun they had jumping up and down on the center of the floor and riding the waves it produced.

The old barn was slowly falling apart and Uncle George felt it a hazard to keep it in operation. Note the lean-to extending from the barn which is partially obscured by the corral in front of the picture. The lean-to was not torn down with the barn, but saved as a milking facility for Uncle George's dairy. Courtesy of the Holtzclaw Collection.

Uncle George and Aunt Georgia often enjoyed ascending the steps to the upper verandah about sunset time. Here one could enjoy an excellent view of the sky that flowered into vivid colors from the sunset. While standing aloft of the verandah there was a view that overstretched the valley floor. Such an experience

Uncle George and Aunt Georgia in front of the Castro Adobe which they had made their home. Note Uncle George holding a large lemon on his prized lemon tree. Courtesy of the Holtzclaw Collection.

was made even more rewarding, because it was being seen from one of the few large adobes remaining from the times of the earliest settlers. It was easy for them to stand there on their elevated perch and look out over the valley, realizing that they were separated by those that once stood there by only a slender thread of history.

After renovation of the interior of some of the bottom level was under firm control, Uncle George now decided to concentrate his efforts of improvement outside the house. He had recently bought a new dodge, and oh, how its beautiful blue color often gleamed in the sunlight, whenever parked near the adobe. Of course with a new car, now his efforts were concentrated on the *cocina* (kitchen) adjoining the house on the north end. He added doors to the room and in general made it like a garage worthy to accept his new car, of which he was quite proud.

The mere mention of this particular garage, however, surely recalls to several a momentous occasion, or at least it was back at that time. Regardless, it is an incident which would perhaps rather be forgotten, but one whose recollection still hauntingly lingers with some. It is perhaps one of the remembrances of the old Castro Adobe with which they could have done without.

Several of the Holtzclaw children had just loaded into Uncle George's car, seated themselves comfortably, and awaited him to take the driver's seat. Aunt Georgia was in the passenger front seat, with Wanda sitting in the center. Several of the others were in the back. Even though the new car was a sedan, and most spacious, they were rather cramped tightly together. This was to be the maiden tour, for the kids had not previously ridden in it. Actually, they were en route to church, a setting that made the little frolicsome act which followed, even less appropriate.

When Rodney set out for the army he left behind several trick, smoke capsules. These items were little cylinders that when electrically ignited made loud noise and emitted smoke. He and his friends around town used to jokingly tie these onto the spark plugs of each others cars. Sometimes they would secretly, obscurely, be nearby awaiting the fireworks that resulted when the friend returned and turned the key to the ignition to start his car, setting off the capsule. Otherwise they would hear about it later, indirectly, and it was always laughable. As youths, they enjoyed doing these pranks.

Anyway, this is where his brother Ken got the idea of placing one of these capsules on Uncle George's beautiful, new, blue car's engine. And as hard as it is to believe today, at that time Ken thought the outcome might be a humorous event. It wasn't! The aftermath would probably have not been so abhorrent if the car had been out in the open air when the capsule ignited. But no, here it was tucked away in this small garage with its immobile atmosphere, with hardly room to open the doors on either side.

So, on this momentous day when all were snugly settled in the car and Uncle George jumped into the driver's seat, Ken leaned back, smiled, and could hardly wait for him to start the car. He had kept it a secret from everyone and had previously sneaked into the garage and installed the trick smoke-bomb to a spark plug under the hood. Uncle George was now anxious to get started, so pushing the key into the ignition slot, turned the key. The result that followed had greatly been underestimated!

Pictured from left are: Ken, Lois, Uncle George, Beverly and Wanda. These were the four Holtzclaw children that often spent visits at the Castro Adobe playing checkers and other games with Uncle George and Aunt Georgia. The old adobe almost became their second home. Courtesy of the Holtzclaw Collection.

Instantly there was a loud bang that in a little garage sounded like a drastic explosion. Then white smoke emitted quickly, streaming from the hood in all directions, and clouding up the garage. It could not have been more of a panic situation than if the car had actually been on fire. In fact, Aunt Georgia screamed aloud, "Fire—get out!"

She was the first one out of the car and scampering through the smoke, followed by Uncle George. Then the next wave followed: first the assembled kids in the back seat, one by one, and then Wanda, who had been sitting in the front seat between the first two evacuees, now somewhat stunned. At this point, Ken was afraid to move, sat there in the car in total silence, hoping to be hidden. Of course this was a dead give away. Why else would he have not been out with the rest, sharing their fright? Uncle George knew that he had the reputation as being somewhat a prankster, and it took him only little time to decipher what had happened.

The next thing heard was Uncle George hollering for his great-nephew to come out of the car and explain himself. Fortunately Uncle George was a forgiving man and after Ken's profuse attempts to apologize he was marched back into the garage. Now the hood was lifted, and Ken obligingly removed the charred culprit and said he was sorry. However, his apology sounded only upon Aunt Georgia's deaf ears, and she was to remain upset for some time. They did make it to church on time, though, but she was quiet all the way. Other than all this excitement, the kids enjoyed the maiden tour of Uncle George's new car and with passage of time the dastardly prank was obscured into oblivion. However, it can be remembered Uncle George telling the story much later at family gatherings, and even getting a rise of humor from family members, except Aunt Georgia, of course. Perhaps the anticipated humor that was originally planned for the christening of uncle's new car came, but a few years late.

The next venture of property improvement undertaken by Uncle George was directed toward the big barn on the grounds near the Castro Adobe. He had decided that it had to be torn down before it fell down, deeming it a real safety hazard. However, the lean-to portion was in good shape, now being used as his dairy barn, and to remain so. It was probably built years after the primary barn.

It was at this time that Uncle George asked Ken if he would take on the job of tearing down his barn, the large portion that was deteriorating. He knew Ken was not afraid of heights, for he had observed him climbing some of the nearby tall trees. Evidently he imagined this youthful energy could be put to better use than tree climbing. And, of course, he could not climb the heights of the roof, and knew Ken was a natural for this task.

The roof was constructed of corrugated metal, consisting of four foot wide by twelve foot sections. These had been nailed to the batten boards extending across the rafters with square nails, all of which were quite rusty. Ken began at the top of the gable on one side, at the upper row of corrugated panels, and began to pull nails, soon finding the claw hammer supplied to him by his uncle almost not required for pulling these antiquated nails; most of them were so loose that they could be removed with fingers. However, once in awhile a nail was found that had out lasted the others, and then the hammer was used. It was almost a wonder that the panels remained intact on the roof.

So this aspect made the task easier, and the activity even actually became fun for the lad on the roof. Each time a panel was loosened, it was allowed to slide down over the undisturbed roof section, and then plunge to the ground. In a manner, it was like watching the old barn slowly disintegrate. On occasion there could be heard Aunt Georgia calling up from the corner of the barn asking if any lemonade was wanted, which was never turned down, even though it involved climbing below to accept it. Tasting so good on hot summer days, it was hard to resist. Aunt Georgia kept everyone supplied with this delicious drink; for Uncle George had planted a lemon tree beside his adobe house, and it now had a bumper crop. She was as proud of the tree as he.

When all the metal was removed, stacked to one side, out of the way, the next segment attacked, was the task of removing the batten boards, those spaced across the rafters to secure the metal sections. They, as well as the metal, came off easily. Nails holding them in place were also rusty and deteriorated. Standing below, one now could see only a rafter skeleton where the roof covering had once been.

Bringing down the rafters at first appeared to be somewhat more tedious. Continuous segments of two rafters running along the length of the barn, rising high from each wall side at a 45 degree pitch, were firmly anchored together by a collar at their junction near the apex of the roof top. This rafter assembly comprised the network of rafter support for the barn's roof. Dismantling the collars high in the air would have been quite a task, especially while balancing high on a ladder while doing so. Ken's big brother Rodney agreed to help with the project, but the travesty was that he was leaving for the army even before the job was begun. But due to Uncle George's ingenuity, the task became rather simple, even though it was done piecemeal. His idea was to stand a ladder vertically, reaching up to the apex of the gable's first rafter section, then tie a rope around that individual section, at its peak. The next step was to remove the ladder, tug on the rope until the section tumbled and swung to the bottom, giving an inverted mirror image of that which was once above. Now the rafter's collar that tied the two rafters could be easily reached and dismantled from below, thereby allowing each rafter to be easily removed from each wall side. However, it was Ken, not Uncle George, who climbed high to to the top of the latter to tie the rope to each rafter segment.

The three walls that remained came down easily; there were only three, because the common wall to the lean-to of the barn was to be left intact, remaining part of the lean-to which was being used for the dairy. Upon dismantling each wall, first the wide vertical boards were pried loose from the wall, cleaned of nails, and stacked in a pile. The heavier, structural studs were easily dropped by pushing over by hand. Ken had immensely enjoyed tearing down this barn, but now gazed at the large pile of residual materials and wondered what Uncle George would do with it all. He wondered what could be done with this material. Uncle George was very happy to have the barn demolished, but did not appear to have any plans for the accumulated materials.

The George Holtzclaw family picture taken at the Castro Adobe one Thanksgiving day. Twenty-three family members shown here lived in or near the Castro Adobe at one time. Courtesy of Virginia McClune Collection.

Alvin was still kept quite busy at his sign shop at Salinas, only about 17 miles away. On week-ends he often tendered his avocado trees that he had planted, some of which were growing quite well. On the other hand, he soon realized that not only frost and gophers were a detriment to his trees, but there was another—it was his boys.

When he was gone during the week they enjoyed nothing more than climbing high to the top of the avocado saplings, to the critical point of equilibrium, and swinging them to the ground. Usually, when they reached that point, the released limb would immediately spring back to its original position when they jumped free. Of course, any broken twigs and leaves were picked up and discarded, so no evidence of climbing was not evident.

On one particular day, however, Gene came down with a crash, as the tree broke at the bottom. Fortunately, he was not injured. He picked himself up, recovered a bit, and walked over to his brother Duane and inquired what he now thought they should do. The concern, of course, was how to explain this damage to their dad. Duane told him he thought they should hide the broken tree. A consensus was soon arrived upon: The boys would carry the broken tree limb over to the southern, not too distant cliff, and toss it over the abyss. Their thinking was if their dad did not immediately see the actual broken tree, maybe the shock would be less.

This was Al's favorite tree, by the way; it was the one that he sometimes walked over to inspect upon coming home from work; it had been growing really well. However, on this particular evening when he drove up the driveway, the void left in the skyline was noticed immediately. Alas, when he walked over to view the mystery, he saw only a trunk stub, and the rest of the tree missing.

The boys, of course, were no where to be seen at that moment, actually in hiding, because they feared a dreaded scenario to follow. Therefore, they put returning to the house off for awhile. Because they had lingered so, it became apparent to their father, without doubt, who had done the dastardly deed. Interrogation began almost immediately when they stepped through the door, both culprits appearing quite downcast. Their father must have felt sorry for them in this dispirited frame of mind, only extracting a promise from them not to climb any more of his trees.

The broken tree was thrown down the same incline where Rodney and Ken once played a dastardly trick on their slightly younger sister, Wanda. It was frightening to her! They told her that they had been riding an old truck tire down the slope by sitting inside it, holding onto the inner rim with both their hands and feet, convincing her that it was great fun, and that she should try it. She accepted the challenge, and away she soon rolled down the hill, with, of course, a strong starting push from her two brothers. Luckily, she missed the trees, fences, and other obstacles along the way. She actually landed in a clump of soft reeds at the bottom of the lowlands. The nearby cows below must have heard the boy's cheering, or perhaps Wanda's screaming, for they stopped their grazing, lifted their heads, and observed. No doubt, they hadn't ever witnessed such an event. Surely, Wanda remembers the episode quite well, even today. Recently the trio visited the old homestead together, and this is one of the several sites they gravitated toward, reminiscing and laughing about that event long passed.

After the barn demolition was completed and the area around all cleaned, Ken sought other jobs from his uncle. By now, because of his exposure to the architecture of the barn and learning about the intrinsic elements incorporated in its construction, he became interested in construction and developed a desire to try his hand at building something; at this point knowing not what, but would attempt anything that came along. Once standing in awe and amazement of the old Castro Adobe, wondering how anyone could attempt to build such a monument, was astonishing. For sure he would not be tempted to construct anything so grandeur. However, at this point he thought there perhaps would never be a chance to build anything.

But fate seemed to intervene, and soon he was busy building a chicken house for his dad, using the old lumber from the barn. He found the construction quite exciting and adapted to it well. The chicken house was intended to be used for three pedigree chickens that his dad was going to buy, two hens and one rooster. His plan was to trap-nest and record the eggs of the two hens; sell the eggs to a hatchery for hatching pedigree strain chickens with previous records. He told his family and son Ken about the plan, how lucrative it was, and Ken became quite interested in joining in and helping with the adventure. Completion of the chicken house was a happy event for everyone. The house was admired by all around, especially after it was painted red using some old paint previously found in the barn. Uncle George stopped by, stood in amazement admiring the beautiful structure, and seemed surprised, but enlightened to know that Ken could actually build as well as demolish. He looked the chicken house over and jokingly declared he felt it not just an average chicken coop, but almost large enough for a small family to live in!

Several weeks after the chicken house was finished a pick-up slip was received from the railroad that the chickens had arrived. Excitedly that evening the chickens were gone after and picked up. They were beautiful White Leghorns, two hens and a rooster packed in a crate and looking quite rail-beaten. The COD charge was paid and it was a surprise to hear the huge amount: $25 for the rooster and $10 apiece for each hen, plus freight charge. They had never heard of such extreme prices for chickens.

One by one, the chickens were released into their new home, and soon the rooster was walking around like he was the "cock of the walk." Two trap nests had been installed which the boy's dad had ordered, and so everyone awaited the next day to see if these great hens would produce as well as advertised. After all, they came from great pedigreed stock, a strain of hens that seldom missed laying an egg each day. The children's grandmother, whom was visiting for the summer months and had previously raised many chickens, walked out to observe the new venture and stated these chickens are sure living "high on the hog." This was one of her favorite expressions.

Alvin Holtzclaw beside the Holtzclaw Neon Company's 35 panel Ford truck, advertising his expertise in sign painting and neon sign making. Courtesy of the Holtzclaw Collection.

Weeks went by and the two hens produced their eggs each day like clockwork. Soon Al was making routine deliveries to the hatchery and happy with the results. The story went well up to this point, but then tragedy struck! Almost in sequence, a fox raided the chicken abode at night and made off with one of the hens and before everyone could absorb this event, a chicken hawk, usually perched high in the nearby big redwood tree, took his toll—the other hen, leaving behind a very excited rooster. Surprisingly, Al took it quite well. Soon he brought home a crate of baby chicks and stated that they may not grow up to be great egg producers like their other hens were but will lay some eggs and make nice Sunday dinners. At this point the children's grandmother took control, secured the grounds against fox and hawk, and did what she really enjoyed—raising chickens. It was not long after she put the rooster on the block with ax in hand. He made a

Alvin Holtzclaw and his son Kenneth proudly stand beside the neon company's truck at the Hansen house residence. The headquarters of the Holtzclaw Neon Company would soon be moved to here from Salinas. Courtesy of the Holtzclaw Collection.

wonderful Sunday dinner for the family, during which time she added a little laughter to the dinner table when she stated they were living "high on the hog", $25 rooster for dinner.

With delight of the successful construction of the chicken house, Ken was spurred to find another building project, which was settled one day when Uncle George mentioned he should use the rest of the barn lumber to build a small barn near his dad's house. Immediately Ken found the idea appealing and after checking with his father, was soon laying out the dimensions for the small barn. His dad was excited about the venture as well, as he had no place for storage except the room under the the-tank water house, and that was limited. Realizing that building a barn was a challenge to him he proceeded with caution, for all he had built up to now was a tree house, several rabbit hutches, and a chicken house.

He somewhat believed that exposure to the architecture of the Castro Adobe and the barn was instrumental in his subsequent acquired fondness for construction. When he used to walk through the massive-walled adobe structure, there always arose an admiration of its construction. It was difficult at this time to view a creation as great as this and not to have a desire kindled within to build,; albeit, though not as grand. In any respect, the adobe structure strongly affected him while living in the proximity of this giant, memorial.

Work on the barn soon began. He staked out the dimensions and planned a small building, one with a flat, but sloping roof. He told his dad the planes and asked his advice, but was informed that he knew nothing about building, and left him to his endeavor. His dad's brother, his Uncle Orville, however, had had some building experience. He stopped by for a visit one day and plans were presented to him, asking for his advice. He greatly encouraged his nephew, gave him some good advice, and before he left confidence was established and Ken was convinced that he could actually build the little barn.

The construction went along well, in spite of the fact that on some occasions someone would have to be tracked down to hold one end of a timber or board while it was nailed. He received lots of advice, little help, for it was looked upon as his own project. Ultimately the barn was under construction and even appeared tangible.

Ken was happy to hear his father say one day that the barn looked good, even though just a framework at this point. He then asked for suggestions of ways it could be put to best use. At this point, Ken had none, and it was only several days later that his dad mentioned a possible application. He suggested he would like to bring over a few bulky items from his neon shop in Salinas to store in the barn's framework, thereby facilitating more room in his shop.

Now in this case, it became imperative to put a firm, elevated, wooden floor in the barn to store items conveniently. This project was soon begun, using more lumber from Uncle George's lumber pile. When completed, his dad began to drag items over, a few at a time. Then he began to even fabricate some of the metal boxes which held the neon tubing and step-down transformers here at this little barn. The sign-box units were the type usually hung near the facade of business buildings. Unaware to Ken at the time, this was the beginning of the new Holtzclaw Neon Company headquarters in Larkin Valley, situated next to the family residence just a short distance away.

A good share of Ken's school's summer vacation was still ahead of him, and he spent much of this time working on improving the sign shop. He was highly elated to have the privilege to do so, as he was enjoying his adventure into the construction arena with a passion, working quite vigorously on the project.

In the interim, more vertical studs were placed here and there, being placed intermittently where felt more were needed; certainly not on the sixteen inch centers construction required today. Of course, at this time there were no building inspections required in this area, and one could construct as it seemed fitting. Then the outside walls were covered with boards and the shell of the building completed.

The days passed by and eventually the building began actually to resemble a workable neon shop. Even before the outside boards were all in tack, his father was moving in some of his equipment and setting up his manifold rack upon the wooden floor that had so meticulously been put together. The final result was impressive and soon arrangements were made for the required electricity to be lined to the building. It was not long after actual bending tubing on the work bench was being done, for now even natural gas was piped to the shop, which was required for torches to heat and bend the neon tubing into signs.

So now, one could watch the total process of making neon signs: First the glass tubing had to be heated and molded into the individual letters to form the specific sign. After that, electrodes were fused onto each end of the sign's hollow tubing. The enclosed array of the sign is now connected to a manifold via a small tube fused both to the sign and the manifold, a check valve separating the two. Previously a drop of elemental mercury is placed into the gaseous passage of the glass tubing of the neon sign, chiefly to induce ionization throughout the neon gas when electrical current is applied across the electrodes, making color array stable.

During this process, when the electrodes of the sign are connected to an electric current from a step-down transformer, then the bombardment process is initiated. At this point, there is seen a dazzling display inside the tubing sign-array similar to a hectic night's electric storm. Al's children can recall watching these bright, dancing, snake patterns, all seemingly headed in different directions. It was exciting for them to observe. Eventually though, after about a day, this action leveled out, and a stable, uniform color was obtained. The sign was now ready for installation.

The natural neon gas colors normally used were red, blue, and orange. But from these three colors, three more could be obtained. When red, blue, or orange neon gas was put into clear glass tubing, whose inner surface was coated with a white powder, then pink, green, and yellow respectively could be obtained. Put into clear tubing, they of course maintained their true color.

Now that neon signs were actually being produced here, the old building in Salinas took second place. It was not too long before a complete move from Salinas was finalized, and the shop there was sold. Al did not have to commute daily to Salinas now, and he enjoyed this atmosphere more among his avocado trees.

Construction came to a lull for awhile, only to be revived the following summer. In the mean time Ken, Wanda and Beverly spent a school term attending a small, church school in nearby Freedom, a small town just north of Watsonville. Next year Ken would be attending a boarding academy, at Lodi, in central California. But the summer between these two events held more adventure for him.

By now Uncle George had done enough renovation in the old Castro Adobe to make it quite livable. But as nice as he made it look, Aunt Georgia was becoming more anxious about the possibility of earthquake while living in the huge building. She had read about the 1906 earthquake and the possibility of one happening again frightened her. Uncle George even went to the extreme of having three large buttresses built on the south wall that had been damaged by the 1906 earthquake, so as to hold the wall from collapsing if this should occur. But this was to no avail, and he was left with the option to move away from the adobe. So he made plans to move from the adobe but to remain nearby.

At this time Al was interested in 40 acres across Larkin Valley Road, directly across from his acreage at the Hansen house. So when Uncle George heard this, he offered to buy the remaining three fourths of Al's acreage, 27.89 acres, so he could build a house to live in on it, and the deal was consummated. Uncle George now added to his land holdings all the land that Al owned between Old Adobe Road and Larkin Valley Road, and land supporting the neon shop, which he also bought However, Al retained title to the Hansen house and acreage around it and continued to live there a short time longer. It was not long until construction was underway for a new house being built for Uncle George on his new property across the street from Old Adobe Road. Upon completion, his happy wife could not put off moving from the adobe another day

When moved in, they appeared quite happy and the children still visited them often. After Uncle George and Aunt Georgia moved out of the adobe into their new house his stepdaughter Larue Vogel and her husband Charles moved into it. They had a son Howard and beautiful adopted twin daughters, Pat and Pam, whom no one could tell apart. Charles was an engineer who worked in Salinas, where he had been involved in mapping out the city. He is the one that brought the head sculpture of Portola and anchored it high on the south wall of the Castro Adobe, where it still remains.

During the Holtzclaw kid's early days at the adobe ranch site they attended Larkin Valley School, which was just a walk over the hill to the school house. Later they attended school at nearby Freedom. Uncle George was a deacon in a local church that had sponsored a private school in Freedom, and it was with his promotion that the children entered this school. They liked it much, and the camaraderie was great. The school included grades up through 9th grade, or first year high school. When Ken finished the eight-grade at Larkin Valley he spent the 9th at Freedom School, along with his siblings of school age. The next year he was to transfer to Lodi Academy, another private school some distance away.

Uncle George was successful in moving Freedom School to be held the next season at Al and Esther's residence, making the large room in front of the house a school class room. This room had once been used as the living room, but the family found it more convenient to locate their living room to a location which once served as a parlor, being easily entered from a side entrance and made really accessible. This made the large room in front of the Hansen house available for a one room school; the next season it was filled with children through early grades up to the eighth grade. Someone humorously noted one time that Al was supplying 80% of the students to the school. Others were Howard Vogel and some living in the local area.

Uncle George was successful in renting the room in the Hansen house from Al, but now he encountered another problem; he needed a nearby place for the teacher, Miss Gerhing, to live. It was around this time that Ken received a real shock, a very unexpected happening. Uncle George approached him to build a cabin for Miss Gerhing to live next to the Neon Shop. Even though he gave much encouragement, Ken hesitated. But after thinking it over and talking to Uncle George in more detail about the project, it began to become exciting; eventually the project was accepted and even though it was quite an undertaking for a 16 year old, it was looked upon with anxiety. Uncle George supplied all the lumber and material that was required during the construction, and his great-nephew again was kept busy building.

When completed it was a personable little cabin, perhaps enough space for one person to live. When Miss. Gerhing moved in she was quite happy. The south view from the window looked down over the bog where the animals grazed and to the west she could enjoy evening sunsets. Uncle George installed water and plumbing, and even brought electricity to the cabin. Her walk to school was just a few steps away, over to the Hansen house. She lived there two years while the school was in session.

The school closed down in 1945 when Al sold the Hansen house to the Hamilton family. Everett and Maude Hamilton and their daughter Virginia moved in immediately after the house was bought. When the Hansen house sold the Holtzclaw family moved directly across Larkin Valley Road to their new 40 acre farm. It was about this time that the Vogel family moved from the Castro Adobe and Uncle George's son Homer and wife Lois moved into it during the time they were building their house off Larkin Valley Road next to Larkin Valley School.

When Virginia Hamilton later married Dale McClune they moved to the little cabin where teacher, Miss Gerhing, lived before she left. But they soon had two children and needed more room, so it was mutually agree upon between their parents and them that they would now switch houses; they would move into the large Hansen house and their parents into the small cabin. This worked well, but much better when the small cabin was moved from its original location to near the vicinity of the Castro Adobe, and made more livable when they added more structural rooms adjoining it. After Virginia's parents died, the renovated cabin became a rental and it remains so today. At this time, Dale McClune assumed proprietorship to the neon shop, and upon his death his son Randy ran the shop, as he does today. Years later, after the Holtzclaw family had moved to the other side of Larkin Valley, they were visiting the Hamilton family with their children. Two of their boys, Gene and Duane, walked out into the avocado grove, which was a reminiscent tour for them, bringing back thoughts when they toppled over their father's prize avocado tree, and the time Maude Hamilton stepped out of her house and hollered at them to get out of those trees; and their defiant calling back to her that they were here first. They remembered these words well and so did Maude Hamilton, for at this exact moment she stepped from the house and in jest yelled out the same words spoken years ago--"You boys get out of those trees."

This brought down laughter from both parties because this was a conversation made years ago which they all remembered so well. Uncle George often told this story at family gatherings and it was always met with humor. He was a great story teller and everyone always loved his humor and he held their interest well. He often told the story about Rod and Ken when they went hunting with their 22-rifles and the result that followed. The story revolved along the following lines and when he told the story it always brought down the house.

Rod and Ken were going hunting and as they hurriedly left the house with guns in hand they grabbed their dad's sack of pipe tobacco to use as a pouch to hold their 22 rifle shells. Loading an adequate amount of shells into the pouch they were off and away on their hunting trip.

The boys planned at the end of their hunt to return their dad's tobacco pouch upon his table next to his favorite chair, thinking it would never be missed, as it was not. The tobacco still remained in the pouch when their dad picked it up after dinner and loaded some tobacco into his favorite pipe and stuffed it down firmly, unaware his boys had used his pouch to carry shells, and upon returning removed all their surplus shells--except one.

Well that evening Alvin leaned back, lighted his pipe and looked forward to a relaxing smoke. The one shell the boys had inadvertently left in the pouch was now in their father's pipe, soon exploding with a large bang, and shattering the body of the pipe into shreds. Alvin leaped from his chair and quickly bolted into the next room. Here he stood, vividly remembering a recent scene of a large grotesque man, lifting his arm with clinched fist, shaking it at him and swearing to shoot him if he was evicted from the property that Alvin was buying. But at the time Alvin was not alarmed and wrote him off as a none threat. So this was the flash back he had, most frightening, thinking all the while he had been shot through the large window he sat by

You know this might not have been so frightening to Alvin had he just thought the pipe had exploded, but alas, here was this frightening flashback of this threatening man, to add to the scene. It had not been long after he bought the property where this occurrence happened when the man refused to move from the premises and threatened him, even though escrow had closed and the property was now Alvin's. The man had to be removed by the sheriff.

Everyone was frightened, but when things settled down solving the mystery of the pipe explosion began. Only the boys at this time eventually realized what had happened but they frightfully remained silent, fearing to bring it to the forefront. It was strange upon investigation to everyone except the boys of the window having no bullet hole or window damage; this definitely ruled out the man shooting at Alvin through the window

Therefore, it was concluded by all except the boys that his pipe must for some reason exploded! Remnants of the pulverized pipe with unnoticed residual pieces of the shell were casually swept away by the two hunters and trashed, and the event of the night was written off as some kind of an unsolved mystery. But what had happened to the lead bullet, the boys wondered about.

It was sometime later that the boy's mother was sweeping in the bedroom adjacent to the family room and swept up the bullet from the shell that fired from her husband's pipe. Alvin was not home at the time but she showed it to her sons Rod and Ken and was concerned from whence it came. At this time they confessed to their mother that they had evidently left a shell in their dad's tobacco pouch after hunting and that he must have loaded tobacco and shell unnoticed into his pipe Their mother laughed, shaking her head in response to the fact that the mystery of the pipe had been solved. Now they looked for the hole where the bullet emitted through the thin 1 inch thick board wall that separated the two rooms, eventually finding a small hole at near ceiling level, having been pierced by the bullet through the board and wall paper.

Mother felt it best not to reveal their findings to their father for awhile and the boys were happy she felt this way. She probably knew that the repercussion would lessen as time passed by, and she was right. In fact as time passed and their father learned what had happened, how the bullet got into his pipe and all that, he had quite mellowed since the incident. He realized that boys will be boys and that it had been an innocent mistake on their part.

This was perhaps Uncle George's favorite story to relate at family functions. At one gathering it was evident that Alvin was totally over the episode when Uncle George related the story to family members in his presence and Alvin laughed louder than most. He did hold his head in jest, though, and exclaim that he still remembered the incident well.

FOUR

By now the Holtzclaw family was living at their new ranch across the way in Larkin Valley. Ken was spending much time away at school, so was only home during the summer season; regardless, during the summer he had time to visit the adobe site often. In 1948 he learned that Uncle George had sold the Castro Adobe to William and Maude Nelson. William Nelson received title to the Castro Adobe and 11.10 acres of land in back of the adobe on November 19, 1948.

In 1948, Ken and his father visited the Castro Adobe and the Nelsons toured them through their proud house, showing them what they had accomplished by now and what they planned to do. Already, it looked quite different from the time when Uncle George owned it. They remembered the Nelsons as being cordial and interesting to talk to. Perhaps the best way to describe the many additions that the Nelsons added to their new home is to quote a typescript of an article by Jeanne Hamilton that appeared sometime later in the Watsonville *Register Pajaronian* on November 5, 1953:

> A historical landmark makes a fine home despite an occasional tourist underfoot. That's what Mr. and Mrs. William M. Nelson of San Francisco discovered during the five years they have lived in the Joaquin Castro Adobe. Known as the "old adobe," it was built in the early 1830's and is closely linked with the history of California.
>
> Mr. and Mrs. Nelson bought the two-story adobe in 1948 because "we fell in love with it." Ever since, they've been slowly adding a few 1953 touches. Each addition has received careful consideration since Mr. and Mrs. Nelson are intent upon keeping the early California atmosphere intact.
>
> The adobe, with a view across low rolling hills to Monterey Bay, is located at 184 Old Adobe Road near Larkin Valley on land once part of the 13,000-acre San Andrés grant. It looks like all restored California missions should, but seldom do. A grape vine at least 75 years old twines its way across the verandah shaded by loquat and lemon trees. Wooden benches and shutters, pots of cacti and pieces of black iron set off the painted white walls. "We hated to paint it, but the rains were destroying the adobe," Mr. and Mrs. Nelson explained. Their house was built by Joaquin Castro, who as a child came with his family to California from Mexico. They traveled with the Anza party and the expedition reached the Pajaro Valley in 1776.

The first home of Joaquin Castro, who was a judge in the Branciforte and Bolada areas in the early 1800's, was in the San Andrés area. He moved across Larkin Valley following trouble with the Indians. The adobe was mentioned by some to be built for Castro's second wife, a Santa Cruz girl of 17. Like the Vallejo 'Glass House" on the south rim of the Pajaro Valley, it also had glass windows.

William and Maude Nelson in the living roon of the Castro Adobe which they had now made there new home. When this picture was taken they were quite settled in the large structure. Courtesy of Nelson Collection

After Castro died there in 1838, his widow married into the Espinosa clan and the family remained at the adobe house. Castro's son, Raphael, who owned the 6,680-acre Aptos Rancho, lived under Mexican and American rule.

In the late 1880's the house was sold to a family by the name of Hansen, but in 1906, following the earthquake, they moved into a house next door. Since then, a series of owners have occupied the historic spot. When Mr. and Mrs. Nelson bought it in 1948, some modern comforts had been installed. "But we've done a lot of fixing up, I can tell you," Mrs. Nelson declared. One of the recent projects has been the electrical wiring system so lights can be turned on by switch instead of pulling a cord. With 30-inch walls, this wasn't easy.

A story has it that the tiles from the roof were sold to a man in Hollywood, but it "may never have had tiles anyway" and so the Nelsons

The living room section showing the staircase that the Nelson family built leading upstairs. Courtesy of Sallie Millang Collection. Courtesy of Nelson Collection.

put on a shake roof after checking to see if it would be in keeping. Roof supports have also been replaced. This fall the San Francisco couple, who spend about four days a week here, had a small floor heater installed in one corner of the living room. "Boulders, each bigger than the last, were taken out in loads. They must have been brought down from the creeks by the Indians," Nelson said. No decay or insect damage was found near the virgin redwood timbers.

Another addition indoors was a set of steps to the second floor using the original stair rail. "Before this the only way to reach the upper floor was by the outside stairway. We think at one time the outside stair faced the other way," said Nelson, who is in the wholesale grocery business in San Francisco. And there are faint markings on the adobe wall to back up his opinion.

When they put in a fireplace several years ago the Nelsons saved the hand- hewn redwood beam from the floor and used it as their mantel. Before, the only way to heat the 30 by 100 foot adobe building was a small potbellied stove. But the thick walls retain heat as well as keep it out. One Indian summer day this fall, it was 65 degrees in the house but out doors the thermometer hit 88 in the shade, 120 in the sunny back path.

Mr. and Mrs. Nelson had a head start on their remodeling job, since previous owners installed closets and cupboards as well as bathroom and kitchen facilities. The original kitchen with big ovens, since walled in, was located where there is now a garage. Outside there was a corral for bull and bear fighting. The redwood trees where grizzlies were tied were chopped down long ago but the Nelsons have found an iron ring to which bears were chained. Mr. and Mrs. Nelson have found some of the original shutters, which they plan to put up at the deep recessed windows.

Inside the house 18 and 20-inch redwood slabs are used for the floor while the ceiling beams are pegged with hand-carved manzanita. Low doorways and deep windowsills are another feature of the adobe. All the doors and ceilings slant-"there's not a straight one in the place," Mrs. Nelson said. Off the living room are the master bedroom and bath with louvered doors. At the opposite end is located the dinning area and small but efficient kitchen where bunches of herbs hung from the ceiling to dry.

Upstairs is where the fandango room, 30 by 50 feet, was once the scene of colorful fiestas. Mr. and Mrs. Nelson are putting in two bedrooms and a large playroom so their two children and four grand children can come to visit. Right now they are debating whether to "clean up" the bedroom walls where generations of children have scratched names and drawing in the adobe. Mrs. Nelson thinks she might like to "tint" the walls slightly to fit in the color schemes. As for repainting the other walls white, the Nelsons have been told they should "age" them by building a big, open fire in the fireplace, letting the smoke sift through the house to get the walls a bit dirty again. Listing the forthcoming projects to be done, Mrs. Nelson says, "We'll do some next year and then keep it up." At present the fandango room hasn't been touched—the partitions still stand, separating it from the dancers' dressing room. It's now stacked high with furniture the Nelsons plan to refinish in their spare time.

Mrs. Nelson, whose mother once owned the famed Winchester House, has always liked antiques and collected them for years before she found the old adobe, a perfect setting for them. In the front room there's a chest of drawers that belonged to General Vallejo who built the "Glass House." Both Mr. and Mrs. Nelson like to paint and their pictures are hanging on the walls. Mrs. Nelson also made colorful rage rugs for the house. The garden surrounding the Castro Adobe has been put in by the couple, and flower beds are edged with adobe bricks. The back yard is still primarily orchard and in the ground can be found iron utensils and pieces of china from years past. In front high up on the wall is the clay head of a man. It's been there for a long time and the Nelsons don't know where it came from or what it represents.

During the five years they have lived in the old adobe the Nelsons have been host to scores of callers and tourists. "People drop in all the time," they report. Included are people whose families once lived there and others interested in the history of California adobe buildings. In restoring their home to its original California setting Mr. and Mrs. Nelson have found there is a feeling of peace and happiness about the place. "And if the ghosts of the early settlers are still around we're sure they are happy ones." Mrs. Nelson said.

The previous quoted article was written in late 1953, approximately six years before the Nelson adobe property was sold. Because of the previous renovation activity accomplished by owner George Holtzclaw, it can perhaps be assumed that the Nelsons were inspired early in the ongoing to continue the quest to make the Castro Adobe even yet more appealing and livable. This they did. However, Mr. Nelson died in 1956 and his widow was nervous about staying alone, so she finally put the adobe up for sale in 1957. Following is an article, titled *Old Castro Adobe up for Sale*, that appeared in the *Register Pajaronian* by the Pajaro Valley Historical Association concerning the sale:

A Pajaro valley landmark--the old Joaquin Castro adobe--along with all of the antique contents, was placed on the market Wednesday noon by the present owner, Mrs. William M. Nelson. More than 120 years old, the huge home sits atop a hill overlooking Monterey Bay, at 184 Old Adobe Way. Its two foot adobe walls still echo the history of another era and its restored beauty adds luster to to the modern homes that nestle about it near the Larkin valley area.

Wednesday noon Mrs. Nelson threw open the doors of this showplace to the public and placed on sale treasures which range from oil paintings to valuable cut glass. For her it spells the end of a nine year residence. The adobe was built for Castro's second wife, a 17-year-old Santa Cruz girl. It was here that Castro died in 1838. Later his wife married into the Espindosa family and retained its ownership until the late 1880s when it was sold to a family named Hansen.

Since then the adobe has passed through many hands. In 1948, the Nelsons saw it for the first time, fell in love with it, and bought it. For the first few years, while they were putting it in order, the Nelsons spent three or four days a week at the adobe, living the rest of the time in San Francisco where he was a wholesale grocer. A year and a half ago Mr. Nelson died. For two months his widow remained at the big adobe house on the hill but finally moved into town and has since resided at the Resetar hotel.

For the past few days the house has been as busy as it must have been when the Castro family lived there. Treasures hidden away in the old fandango room--unused since its old Spanish service as a ballroom--were hauled out and cleaned up. Antique furniture was dusted off and moved into the huge living room. Mrs. Nelson, whose mother owned the famous Winchester house, has collected antiques for years. She found the old adobe the perfect setting for them.
Wednesday morning she prepared for the sale of these items, her brunet beauty giving her the look of a Spanish *senora* who awaited the arrival of guests rather than curious customers.

The house is being priced at approximately $35,000. It has been strengthened by its current owner with concrete abutments. A heavy shake roof was added to replace the old one which rumor says was purchased by a Hollywood contractor.

There is a fireplace at the end of the living room. At the opposite side there is the dining room and kitchen and a stairway leading to the second floor where two bedrooms were created from a small part of the long entertainment hall known as the fandango room. Where once the old Castro Adobe was the center of activity for a part of the 13,000 acre San Andrés grant, today it still retains 12 acres of land--much of which has been cut up to make room for modern houses erected in the vicinity. Mrs. Nelson has no plans for the future. When the antiques are sold--when the furniture is moved out--and when the house acquires new owners--then, she says, she will make up her mind about her own future. But not until then, she emphasized. Another landmark will have changed hands!

Then in November 7, 1957, another article came out in the *Register Pajaronian*, titled--*Old Adobe Up for Sale: Historical Group Wants It*, and is given by courtesy of the *Castro Adobe Archives*. It expresses that the Pajaro Valley Historical Society and others were concerned about purchasing the property. However, it was later learned that the visit by the Pajaro Valley Historical Society never came about. Regardless, the article follows below:

>The old adobe of the Rancho San Andrés--last Spanish adobe in tact between Monterey and Santa Cruz and perhaps the sole existing historical marker in the entire area--was being eyed this week by other interested local historians. The Pajaro Valley Historical society's directors and county officials will have a look at the adobe sunday afternoon, and consider their chances of acquiring and preserving it as a showplace and museum.
>
>The adobe, home of the Castro family which held the San Andrés ranch grant since 1833, has been preserved and modernized as a residence. Located near Larkin Valley road its now on the market, the historical society learned--and the society has long sought to preserve one of the historic old buildings as a museum of local history. The society met opposition some years ago in a nearly-successful campaign to reconstruct the famed Vallejo "Glass House" on Werner's hill. After the state park commission showed reluctance to take the property over, the ravages of weather reduced it to a virtual ruin.
>
>The Castro Adobe, however, has been kept in a fine state of preservation, the president Mabel Rowe Curtis of the historical society said, and ought to be acquired by the county or state as a historical monument. Three land grants were given the Castro family by the Spanish crown in 1833, lying along the shore of Monterey bay from Soquel creek

to the mouth of the Pajaro river. The southern part of the ranch which includes the house was occupied for 10 years by the father, Joaquin Castro, a pensioner soldier who came with Anza to the village of Branciforte (now Santa Cruz), where he was alcalde in 1831. The Rancho San Andrés of two square leagues (some 8,000 acres), was conformed to his eldest son, Guadalupe, in 1876. The adobe was the second home built on the rancho, with a sweeping view over the valley to Fremont's peak. Its main room was 25 by 50 feet. A large grapevine, planted more than 120 years ago, still stands across the front of the building.

The Nelson widow sold the adobe late in 1959 to John and Suzanne Paizis, past owners of a smaller adobe in Monterey, but now looking for a lager one to buy. While house hunting in the area an ad was seen by them in the *Register Pajaronian,* in Watsonville. They had been looking for something near the ocean in Santa Cruz, but little was available. So when the ad turned up and they liked living in adobes, they decided to take a look. When they turned into the driveway from Old Adobe Road, looked at each other and said, "This is it." They spent no time in buying the property. They received title to the Castro Adobe on October 2, 1959. The rest is history.

And the rest was history because a number of other families inhabited the old adobe after them in the forthcoming years. During these future years each took their turn in further adding to the renovation of the Castro Adobe making it even more livable. The picture above of the staircase in the living room of the Castro Adobe was very impressive to several of the Holtzclaw children when they visited the Nelson's abode, for when they used to visit their Uncle George and Aunt Georgia in the Castro Adobe, it was not yet constructed. It certainly shows how much work the Nelsons did on the property.

FIVE

The following chapter about John and Suzanne Paizis and their short stay living in the Castro Adobe was of great interest to the author to compile. He had met them several years ago when Suzanne was writing her book about the Castro Adobe and they became good friends. She interviewed him at the time and he supplied her with a section about his remembrances of the Castro Adobe for her book

On October 2, 1959, John and Suzanne Paizis received title to the Castro Adobe and were anxious to move into it as their residence, which they soon did. Perhaps it is best to introduce them via the following 1959 article, *Champions of Adobe Tradition Buy Castro Adobe,* that appeared in the *Register Pajaronian*, a story about the new couple that arrived there and bought the Castro Adobe. The article follows:

> The Joaquin Castro Adobe at 185 Old Adobe Road in the Larkin Valley which has had a varied history during its more than 120 years of existence has new owners. Sale of this link with the early Spanish-American history of the Pajaro Valley to Mr. and Mrs. John Paizis was announced this week. The property was sold to the couple, new arrivals in Santa Cruz county, by Mrs. Maude Nelson, who has owned it since 1948.
>
> Paizis, a psychologist, this year joined the staff of the Santa Cruz county superintendent of schools. He and his wife and two children of kindergarten and seventh grade age have been living in their new home a month. Ownership of an adobe home is not new to the Paizises. In fact Carmel Valley, where they lived recently, they bought an adobe—not an old one Mrs. Paizis says. It consisted of one large room and a kitchen. Paizis built on two bedrooms, maintaining the original style and even making his own adobe bricks.
>
> Paizis' assignment to the Santa Cruz county school system is his first after having completed his internship at Children's Health Council in Palo Alto. Prior to that, he taught school for five years, a requirement for his Psychology degree. His teaching experience included schools in Carmel and Daly City. Mrs. Paizis also is a teacher, taught last year in the Carmel Valley school system.
>
> Once again the Castro Adobe is undergoing some renovation. Mrs. Paizis is wielding some paint brushes and putty knives, but she said no major changes in the building are planned. "We'll maintain the simple

style of the home," She said. Mrs. Nelson and her husband, the late W. Nelson of San Francisco, made the last major modernization of the home, but they too strove to keep its original style. Since her husband's death, Mrs. Nelson has lived at the Resetar hotel.

The adobe is known to have been built in the early 1830's by Joaquin Castro, who as a child of six came with his family to California from Mexico. His first home was in the San Andrés area, but he was reported to have moved across Larking Valley following trouble with

John and Suzanne paizis in 1963 when they lived in the Castro Adobe. Courtesy of Suzanne Paizis Collection.

Indians. The adobe was built for Castro's second wife, a Santa Cruz girl of 17. Like the one time "Glass House" on Werner's hill, it had glass windows. After Castro died there in 1838, his widow married into the Espinoso clan. Castro's son, Raphael, who owned the 6,680-acre Aptos rancho, lived under Spanish, Mexican and American rule.

In the 1880's the house was sold to a family by the name of Hansen, but in 1906, following the earthquake, they moved into a house

View of the back garden of the Castro Adobe the Paizis family loved so dearly. They labored many hours to bring it to this perfection. Courtesy of Suzanne Paizis Collection.

nearby. Before its purchase by the Nelsons, there had been a series of other owners. Recently the Pajaro Valley Historical association had expressed interest in purchasing the Castro Adobe. However, the project was too large for the association's limited funds. Sale of the home was handled through the Edward A. Hall & Son real estate agency.

John and Suzanne Paizis had bought an Adobe whose first floor had already been renovated, but the fandango room upstairs needed much attention. The large upstairs room had not yet been divided, other than the two bedrooms established there by previous owner, the Nelsons. However, the rest of the upstairs was closed off at this time. When John and Suzanne walked into the closed off area in the fandango room they found it more like an attic or barn. If they were to add more rooms to the upstairs, then stabilizing it was a priority, as the floor was a trampoline—it bounced.

At this point, stabilizing the upper floor was top priority before they could expand living quarters there. Prior to supporting the floor, when they watched television in the closed off fandango room and the dogs were there, when they scratched the whole place rattled as if there were a minor earthquake, with no feeling of stability at this time at all.

Because of this instability, before any more rooms were to safely be built upstairs, John and Suzanne deemed it prudent to first support the floor, which badly needed to be supported. When the Nelsons built the upstairs bedrooms, they supported the immediate area of the two bedrooms by installing steel cables from the roof to hold the floor up. Because this seemed to work well, the Paizis' chose this method. When all the steel cables were installed the Paizis' were able to add rooms that they could use. Also they could sheet rock over the cables, concealing them.

Then there arose another problem when they put in the master bedroom upstairs, which was 15 feet by 50 feet; there were gaping holes in both corners of the room, cracks that they assumed were associated with the 1906 earthquake, because they were not normal kinds of gaps from aging. As the walls were nearly three feet deep, the openings were at least a foot wide on the inside, but did not extend through to the exterior. The author remembers seeing these wide gaps as a kid when he often frequented the fandango room and wondered what caused them, not being aware then of the 1906 earthquake. He like many before him enjoyed carving his initials in the inside adobe walls of this room. S u z a n n e solved the problem of the cracks; she mixed mud and carted it up in buckets and patched up the gaps, plastering and smoothing them over. When painted everything looked fine, and no further cracks appeared during the years they were there.

Other changes upstairs done by the Paizis' included a sewing room, a fourth small bedroom, and redwood panels in the master bedroom and redwood ceilings in both rooms. The original wall partition originally blocking off the unused area was left in tact, and the wall was brought all the way to the ceiling. Double louvered doors to the master bedroom were installed. Sheet rock divided and covered the cabling, as was the case in the Nelson bedrooms.

The next major task that the Paizis family attempted was removing the posts on the front verandah, as they were full of termites and dry rot. They had identical posts hewn by hand. When the old posts were replaced there were old Concord grape vines which grew on them perhaps 75 years old or older; they were picturesque as previous pictures might show, and even though an effort was extended to save them, they never grew back, which was sad. New Concord grapes were later planted. The balustrade was still in good condition and there was no need to replace it.

Prior to this time the balcony deck was rebuilt as well as the outside staircase. When the shaky staircase was rebuilt its direction was changed. Along

View of the cocina/carport wall in June 1968. John Paizis decoraed the wall with found objects. Courtesy of Suzanne Paizis Collection.

the outer plastered adobe wall, one could see an imprint of stairs that had formerly risen in the opposite direction. The outline was quite recognizable. The stairs are very steep in the early 1889-90 Hansen photograph, rising from bottom left to top right, while the 1895 photo of the Hansen family shows no stairs at all. This is quite strange, because this would allow no entrance to the upper floor, as there was no inside staircase at this time to the upper floor. The Paizis' built their staircase to coincide with the old imprint in the adobe wall, although less steep, rising from bottom right to top left. This gave better ground floor access, since one would always be covered by veranda when going from the front door to the stairwell.

The Paizis' also made changes outside the adobe, tearing down the old two-story wooden water tank that stood across from the front door. It was picturesque, and if not in bad shape would have made a nice studio but it was rickety, full of dry rot and termites. Restoring it was not of high priority, so it was torn down. The author stopped by to see the old adobe home site one time around the early 1960's and noticed that the water tank was gone, starring in awe at the vacant spot. To him it was one of the great landmarks of the area and its disappearance saddened him. No one was home at the adobe, so he did not meet the Paizis family members at that time to inquire about the water tank, but later learned from Virginia McClune that they had to destroy it because it became a hazard due to termite damage. His memories of the old water tank still lingered from his childhood, however.

Back in the house, a new sink, plumbing, and electric range and electrical wiring were included in the Paizis renovation. Because the kitchen floor was badly in need of restoration—black and white linoleum was laid on the floor. In the bathroom, there were two matching washbasins and two large mirrors installed and the old metal shower stall was replaced with a proper tub, adding a new decorative green and white Mexican tiles. Blue and yellow Mexican tiles went on the kitchen cupboards while blue, yellow and terra cotta tiles framed the front door.

A door between the present kitchen and the garage, ex-*cocina,* was carved out of the block wall, as it was desirable to have direct access there rather than having to go outdoors to do so. Also, this made the second bathroom in the garage easily accessible as well. To accomplish this fete, part of a three-foot thick wall had to be removed between the kitchen and the garage. When the outline of the door was sawed through with a lumberjack saw and the bricks were carefully removed, there were chicken prints on one brick, formed in the 1830 or thereabouts. Evidently, when the brick was drying, a chicken had run over it. There were also some handprints of people who had made and carried the bricks as well. It was a very thought-provoking event for the John and Suzanne Paizis to see these signs of life that were at the time over a hundred and twenty years old. The task became a case of archaeology as well as removing bricks for a door.

When John and Suzanne lived in the adobe the story that the Castro family had buried a large cache of gold still existed. Once a friend, Dr. Duncan Holbert visited when metal detectors were first popular. Duncan's son Mac went over the area picking up sounds from metal items, hoping to find the gold. He found square nails, horse shoes, and other related items. Once there was a great chatter from his detector just behind the back door of the house. It was exciting because it chattered so much. Aha, Eureka, we have found the gold, he exuberantly thought. They started to dig.

Well, it took some time to dig down the few feet while the detector chattered on. Finally they unearthed a rusty old range which had been discarded and buried just outside the kitchen door. Who would have expected anything like that? Their excitement subsided, and they just covered the range back over. The author is sure he would have been just as excited if this had happened back when he lived so nearby, for stories at that time of Joaquin's gold persisted.

The Paizis family paid twenty-six thousand dollars for the adobe in 1959 after the house had been on the market for a number of years. At the time, the Pajaro Valley Historical Association was interested in buying it. They often rented it for events and meetings. Particulars are unknown why the historical society never bought it. At this time there was a chicken ranch across from the adobe. When the author lived there it was all open fields where the chicken ranch was now. At the roads end a farmer, John Fiorovich, had a chinchilla ranch and owned the apple orchard between the adobe and his chinchilla ranch. John and Suzanne used to walk around the apple orchard, joined by all their dogs and cats.

Hearing this was reminiscent for the author for this was one of his favorite walks when he lived in the Hansen house. Then, the ranch up the road was owned by Mr. Thompson, who raised large Berkshire hogs, quite a contrast from chinchillas. He also operated the apple orchard. Before the Holtzclaw family moved away, Al Dempster, the cartoon artist for Walt Disney moved to the Thompson place. He set up a studio and drew cartoon cells which he sent to Walt Disney Studios to be incorporated into those short cartoons, the ones often seen at the beginning of movies during that time.

The renovation the Paizis family did for the adobe inside the house was totally matched by the front and back yard improvements. The swimming pool added a great atmosphere to the yard and garden. The large loquat tree in the front made the adobe structure stand out so beautifully, or in the back yard, the beautiful blue clematis vine that Suzanne planted, which climbed above to the high roof so graciously, extending its array of color along its pathway added even more to the beauty. When daughter Varvara was misfortunate of having rheumatic fever during the spring of her first year in kindergarten she often sat in the wide adobe window sill on a pillar, admiring the beautiful engrossment of purple clematis. It was here that she was drawn so close to nature. Outside the window at eye level she watched a hummingbird build its little soft nest and lay its tiny white eggs. In the little window seat she sat day after day, stilled by her illness, and witnessed the cycle of nest building, birth, and nurturing. When the eggs hatched, the little hummingbirds looked more like worms than birds. Little open beaks eagerly awaited their mother's cache of nector. One day the little birds were gone, completing a lovely segment in a little girl's life.

The adobe and property, beautiful as it was, became too difficult for John and Suzanne to care for. So shortly after Suzanne's daughter, Melanie, was born in 1962, the family sold the house and started a new adventure in Rio Del Mar, Aptos, California.

On April 24, 1963, the Castro Adobe was conveyed to Vic and Sidney Jowers from the Paizis family, although they did not take possession until late in June. The Jowers had become friends with the Paizis family, getting to know them because they at times had a dinner at their restaurant, the Sticky Wicket, on Highway 1. When they mentioned that they were going to sell the adobe because they were expecting a baby and thought it would not be wise to have both a young child and an outside balcony, Vic and Sidney became interested in buying it.

SIX

The Jowers family was planning to move from their apartment below the restaurant to a larger place and they loved the adobe. Sidney's brother Clifford and wife Ann in New York shared in the purchase. The four of them bought the property together and Clifford and Ann, with their children Anne and Paul, the same ages as Vic and Sidney's children, Laura and Andrew, drove out each summer to stay during school holidays. They shared the house and Clifford used it as both gallery and painting studio. Below is a newspaper article from the Watsonville *Register-Pajaronian*, Thursday, December 9, 1965, by Winefred R. Gauvrea, which was written some time after the Jowers moved into the adobe:

> The present owners, Victor and Sydney Jowers, purchased the house in 1963. A few more coats of white paint have been added for further protection of the old walls, and lots of wax to the old floors which are made of 18 and 20 inch redwood planks. Another special note of interest is the beaded ceiling beams pegged with hand carved manzanita. The low doorways and deep window sills are another feature no longer seen. They have plans for further improvements but are moving slowly. There are many things they'd like to do but it is all costly. Still remaining to shade the front is a magnificent old loquat which was planted long after Joaquin Castro and his bride moved in. Also remaining is the legend of a buried treasure of Spanish doubloons. The Jowers however believe it is nothing more than the weaving of imagination formed over the years as the original grant was whittled away from its original 13,000 or more acres to the remaining 10 surrounding the house.

The first improvement the new owners made after they moved in was to replace the earth floor in the original kitchen area, used at the time as a garage, to control the dust that was constantly tracked through the doorway the Paizis family had cut through the outside wall into the present kitchen/dinning room. With the new floor, Vic now had a dust-free outside place for her laundry.

The Jowers greatly enjoyed the grounds around the adobe and they liked living in the countryside. They wanted to open up the back field and hillside for walking and just to have it accessible. They engaged a person to cut out and grade a road winding down behind the redwoods to the valley below, so if they wanted to have a cottage or camp down there they could, and their children could play there. Sometime during the 60's when the author visited the adobe home site he walked this new road and thought how great it was! This would have been a blessing for him and his siblings when they lived in the Hansen house, for they had to take a round about path to get down to the valley below, which was called the bog. There was a nice creek running through the bog, and they spent many hours there as kids.

The Jowers knew that a friend of the Paizis family had covered the

From left: Victor, Laura, Andrew and Sidney Jowers in 1963 when they purchased the Joaquin Castro Adobe. Courtesy of Sidney Jowers Collection.

surrounding ground with a metal detector, in search of the Castro's cache of buried gold, but had not touched the adobe walls. So the Kings, friends of theirs, were invited to come over with their metal detector and go over the walls, which they had great fun doing. The children of the King's family and Sidney's family were very excited at the prospect of finding treasure, but nothing turned up, only old license plates and chicken wire used in plastering.

The three large buttresses to the end wall were a mystery to the Jowers, but they had heard they were added to the Castro Adobe just after the 1906 earthquake to give necessary support to the damaged wall. This is true in a way; the three buttresses were built to give support to the wall alright, but were constructed much later than "just after" the 1906 earthquake. The author personally watched them being constructed some time in the late 1940's when his Uncle George was having them installed. He was told by him at the time that he was having this done so his wife would not worry about the end wall falling down.

During the time the Jowers family lived in the adobe, they held numerous social functions. In 1967, Saturday, September 23rd, they held the Cabrillo Music Festival at their home, listed on the program as—*An Evening at the Old Adobe*. They used the balcony of the adobe as a minstrel's gallery for gala events they held there, usually as fund raising for the Cabrillo Music Festival. Sidney Jowers and Suzanne Paizis hosted events like this sometimes together at the Castro Adobe.

Initially, Sidney and Suzanne were members of the inaugural board for the festival, Suzanne as president and Sidney as the organizer for the Art Exhibition that was part of the first two years' events. These were held in the Carrillo's library and adjoining patio. The idea of the festival grew from the evening concerts at the Jowers' Sticky Wicket restaurant that Bob Hughes initiated after he came to Aptos to study composition with the composer Lou Harrison. Lou Harrison was a good friend of the Jowers family and when he knew they were moving into the Castro Adobe, he immediately offered to bring over his 1871 Steinway grand piano, one that had came here around the horn. It fit beautifully in the large living room of the adobe, and was adored by many friends and visitors.

In 1968 a Renaissance party was hosted by Sidney Jowers and Robert Hughes in the grounds and gardens of the Castro Adobe. The event included many guests and musicians from around the area, including the Jowers' good friend Lou Harrison, a well known American music composer. Mr. Harrison lived his first nine years in Portland, Oregon, where he was born in May 14, 1917. Since then residences included numerous places, including Central California, Los Angeles, New York City (ten years), North Carolina, the San Francisco Bay region, Oaxaca, New Zealand, and the Monterey Bay region where he currently lived. He is the recipient of several grants and awards, including Guggenheim and Rockefeller Fellowships. Mr. Harrison has established himself as one of the most original and important American composers of the 20th century.

Party-goers gathered on the patio lawn to eat by candlelight while Renaissance music was played from the balcony which runs along the entire length of the adobe. The adobe supplied a great atmosphere for such events. Soon after this event it was announced that the Jowers family was going to soon move to England.

When Sidney was asked how she thought use of the adobe property should be used if the proposed responsibility of the adobe was to be assumed by the state, as expected, she said that she saw no reason why the combined use as a museum and use of special events could not been combined. She said she thought the adobe should be a museum, open to the public, with events throughout the year, preferably musical events. It's a wonderful space to hang paintings, so exhibitions could be considered. Just before Sidney Jowers moved to England, the *Santa Cruz Sentinel* presented an article in their paper, by Margaret Koch, describing the Renaissance party, somewhat of a farewell party given by Mrs. Jowers, a farewell to all her friends, entitled —*Historic House…A Farewell Party*:

> Out on Old Adobe Road , in the San Andrés area of Santa Cruz County near Watsonville, there sits a handsome old adobe house that is more than 125 years old. It was the home of Don Joaquin Castro. This house, currently the home of Mrs. Victor Jowers and her children, Laura and Andrew, was the scene of a Renaissance party—a sort of farewell party given by Mrs. Jowers who will leave soon for England. The party served a two-fold purpose: Mrs. Jowers' farewell to the old adobe which is to be sold, and as a gathering of a group of artist who met through the Sticky Wicket. Mrs. Jowers and her late husband formerly operated the "Wicket" which became an Aptos center for art and the performing arts.
>
> The party featured 15th-18th Century music played by Diva Goodfriend-Koven, flute, Dorothy Isaacon, oboe, and Doug Isaacon, bassoon. Food was served in the garden-patio by candlelight and was arranged to depict a Renaissance still life painting. Guests wore long gowns and clothing suggestive of the Renaissance period. Robert Hughes, who served as host for the gathering, notes that it represented the "end of an important period in the development of the arts in Santa Cruz County."
>
> The adobe was constructed sometime in the mid-1830s; the exact date is unknown. It was the second home built by Joaquin Castro, a pensioned soldier who had arrived at Monterey in the schooner *Concepcion* in 1799. He built it for his second wife, Rosaria Briones, a bride aged 17. The house is 30 by 100 feet in size; the upper floor originally featured a ball-room 30 by 50 feet.

In 1880 the old adobe house was purchased by the Hansen family; in 1948 it passed into the hands of the William Nelsons and some modern comforts were installed. The Nelsons had it re-wired for electricity, a fireplace and an inside stairway built. They also turned the ball-room into two bedrooms.

The John Paizis family bought it in 1959 and made further improvements, including modernizing the kitchen. Five years ago the

The party that was held at the Castro Adobe which was a farewell given by the Jowers family. Courtesy of Jower Collection.

Jowers' bought the house. They painted it inside and out, helping preserve the thick adobe walls; they also added layers of wax to the glossy redwood plank floors.

Out in the front garden stands a magnificent old loquat tree, a survival of the days when Joaquin and his young bride lived there. An old legend says there is buried treasure there too—Spanish doubloons. The nine acres on which the house now stands was once a part of the Rancho San Andés, granted to members of the Castro family in 1833.

David and Elizabeth Potter purchased the adobe from Sidney Jowers on July 10, 1968, becoming a second home to them. Elizabeth was a Fellow of the California Historical Society.

SEVEN

David and Elizabeth Potter were very happy with their purchase of the Rancho San Andrés Castro Adobe in 1968. Since Elizabeth's father, George Lyman was a California historian and author, Elizabeth was always interested in having an adobe of her own. So when another member of the historical society mentioned the Castro Adobe being on the market, she and David journeyed to Watsonville and they realized the house "was right up their alley."

David Potter in front of the Castro Adobe. Note that the butresses no longer are against the south end wall as previously seen. Courtesy of the Potter Collection.

When the Potters first moved in their top priority was to reshape the garden area outside the adobe. They called in the landscape architect Thomas Church to create a garden in the original Spanish-Mexican style. The raised swimming pool in the rear garden, built by the Paizis family and enjoyed by the Potters, was demolished, as well as the three buttresses against the damaged south-end wall from the 1906 earthquake.

Church proceeded to redesign the garden at the rear of the house. He placed the St. Francis statue, which Maude Nelson bought in the 1950s, in the center of the garden and designed paths around it. He brought in olive trees and plants of the type that could be found in mission gardens. Elizabeth wanted a fragrant garden and one that hummingbirds would enjoy. He also put in the adobe walks under the front veranda and in the back of the house. The bricks were made in Modesto, especially for the house. They wanted it to look rustic like old bricks and these bricks made it look that way.

Elizabeth Potter in front of the Castro Adobe in 1968, the year she moved into the house. Courtesy of Potter collection.

In 1974, David built the doors to enclose the *cocina*, which had been used as a garage by former residents. The old doors were of picket fence material but the new wood came from railroad ties that had formerly been on the Oakland Bay Bridge; the second deck had been for trains and some years ago when they were building BART, they removed the railroad tracks and took off the ties to make way for BART. They were old twelve by twelve redwood timbers—big. They made a lot of pieces of wood out of them at Beard's Sawmill in the Ferndale district on Brown's Valley Road. The old redwood was used in many local homes, and David made the doors for the *cocina* out of some of it.

A major undertaking however was the drilling of a new well, because the other one went dry. They got Nick Pavlovich out there because he told them he was a water witcher and they needed to know where to have the well drilled. He walked all around the place and right on the other side of the fence; away from the house to the west about 200 feet from the road he found the spot to drill their well. So the well driller went down about three hundred feet and found water. They built a little post adobe shed that held a new pressure tank with a water filter, and the water problem was solved.

Soon the Potters realized that the floors on the bottom floor had to be rebuilt, especially one day when David broke through the floor in the living room. That old floor was built right on the ground and that is why the boards rotted. The potters contacted Val Panzich of the Watsonville Construction Company and he went right to work on the project. He took all the old wood out and rebuilt it with boards about fourteen to fifteen inches wide. They were redwood boards and hard to find. New joists were installed as well, which involved some excavation, because the other joists were laid directly on the ground. After this renovation to the floor, the roof was looked at and determined to need new shakes, which they had a roofer do. At the same time they braced the rafters and reinforced the cables that held the second floor up.

Soon after this project, another project was begun; a bathroom, water heater and tub were installed upstairs. To hide plumbing and electrical wires, they were run through downstairs cabinets. Some went through the downstairs book case and cabinets next to the fireplace.

It was in 1986 when David brought in an architect. He looked at the damage to the south wall from the 1906 earthquake and decided it needed some reinforcement to guard against possible damage from any future quake. He put a new foundation at the south end with piers underneath every twenty feet and lateral bond beams to another pier out about ten feet. He went down twenty feet and put in reinforcing steel, which was done in sections and dug three or four feet at a time. It was quite a structure. It should stay there forever; it will really hold the wall up now, they thought.

David and Sidney Potter were very interested in the history of the adobe, so they ordered the Historic American Building Survey Inventory of the adobe, which was recorded June 10, 1972, to see if they could find additional history about it. The recorder was Rebecca Lynn Manhood, a student of the University of California. The document received is depicted below:

The oldest part of the Castro Adobe, the one-story *cocina* on the northern side, was probably built sometime between 1338 and 1844 by Joaquin Ysidro Castro, who is thought to have come to California as a member of Juan Bautista Anza's party about 1776. The larger two-story dwelling which adjoins the *cocina* on its western side was probably built by Joaquin's son Juan Jose, a few years later, between 1847 and 1852. There are records of Joaquin's ownership of the land in 1823, authorized by Governor Jose Figueroa, and again the adobe in 1833. Juan Jose was recorded in town records as occupant of the big adobe in 1852 until 1874 when his mortgage was foreclosed. The land was occupied at various

A Certificate of Recognition presented to Mr.&Mrs. David Potter from the Santa Cruz Hiatorical Trust, March 1987. Courtesy of the Potter Collection.

times also by Indians, which artifacts found around the house suggest. There was a long history of ownership that followed Juan Jose's. By 1915, the building had degenerated into a hay barn and storage space until it was finally restored several years later. The present owners, Mr. and Mrs.

David Potter of San Francisco, have occupied the Castro Adobe for about three years.

The building is a fine example of the early Californian house which was prevalent from about 1835 to 1845 in the period of Mexican influence. The buildings have thick, white-washed adobe walls and wooden shingle roofs which were originally baked tile. The main two-story building is approximately one-hundred feet long and thirty feet deep; the *cocina* about thirty-five by thirty feet. It has a typical second-story veranda with stairs on the western side, which were originally the only means of reaching the second level. The house is long and flat, and the rooms were originally long with fewer walls than at present. The thin balusters of the veranda and the chamfered posts in front and back are unusually delicate refinements for this style of house. All original materials were locally obtained.

Prior to David and Elizabeth Potter selling of the adobe to Joseph and Edna Kimbo, they received a well deserved Certificate of Recognition, March, 31, 1987, awarded by the Santa Cruz County Historical Trust in appreciation for outstanding achievement in historic preservation and extensive stabilization work to preserve the historic 1840s Castro Adobe. They were happy to receive this award, shown above, and considered it a great recognition of their efforts while living at the Adobe.

EIGHT

In August of 1988, the sale of the Castro Adobe to Joseph and Edna Kimbro was finalized and they soon moved into the adobe. Shortly afterwards they were outside and the kids came running out of the house yelling that the whole upstairs room was shaking even more when they ran over it. Their parents calmed them down by saying that there was nothing to worry about. They later learned from the USGS that this motion was the precursor of the Loma Prieta earthquake.

Their youngest son Joey, really loved living in the adobe. He liked having his friends there and they had beautiful birthday parties in the garden. They would climb trees and play on the balcony. They liked to play in the fandango room, the big room upstairs. They would run all around it and really had fun playing there. They especially liked the way the floor swayed from side to side when they ran across it.

Edna was gone from January to June of 1989 when she was gone to Rome. She learned she had to speak Spanish in order to study what she wanted, so she came home in June and enrolled at UCSC to learn Spanish. Then the Loma Prieta earthquake hit in October 17, 1989, deeming the adobe house unlivable. Therefore, the family actually did not live in it very long. The Loma Prieta earthquake was directly witnessed by Edna Kimbro at the adobe, the only adult that witnessed the event. I think the best way to reveal the story about the earthquake at the adobe then is to hear in her words of what happened that day. Below is given her rendition of the story as later related to Suzanne Paizis, January 28, 2001 in an interview for Suzanne's book, *The Joaquin Castro Adobe in the Twentieth Century—From Earthquake to Earthquake*:

> I had just returned from picking up my oldest son, David, from school. I opened up the house and he put his schoolbooks down in the kitchen on the counter next to the sink. I was going back to pick up my other son Joey, who was at day care, when David, instead of staying in the kitchen to get a snack, followed me out to the doorway of the garage (*cocina*) to say something to me. I already had the ignition on in the Ford Ranger truck, which was parked in front of the *cocina*, and all at once the truck started moving violently from side to side as it were going to tip over. I couldn't figure out what was going on. My son was trying to say something to me from the doorway.

I finally got out of the car and realized it wasn't the car that was moving; it was the ground. I was some distance away from David and tried to get him away from the doorway because the doorway is very wide but doesn't have a lot of bearing for the lintel above. I was afraid that the way the building was moving, the *cocina* would go in one direction, fall

Happy days at the adobe home prior to the 1989 earthquake that destroyed part of their home. Courtesy of Kimbro Collection.

on him, and because it was very heavy, kill him. But I couldn't get to him fast enough. I was yelling, "Get out!" David had been taught at school to stand in a doorway but the ground was moving violently and the pepper tree was whipping around as I stood there. I finally got him out of the doorway. This went on for seventeen seconds, a long time. I was convinced it was the apocalypse! Then I thought, "No, it's an atomic bomb—we were done for!" Then I looked down and a crack opened up in the ground beneath my feet. It went toward the low adobe wall, past the loquat tree, and over to the adobe pavement and right up the wall to the window, and from the corner of the window all the way to the top of the building. I saw it happen! And I thought, "This is an earthquake! It isn't the end of the world, it's an earthquake!" I heard a horrible noise and looked at the opposite end of the building and there was like a mushroom cloud of brown. The upper portion of the south end of the building collapsed and the huge cloud that came up in the air was adobe.

The view of the Castro Adobe as it appeared in June of 1996, prior to 2002 when interest by the state was kindled to make it a park. Courtesy of the Holtzclaw Collection.

It was at that point the burglar alarm, which has two different horns, started blaring and continued for about an hour. We couldn't figure out how to stop it. There were aftershocks in addition to a very high power pole quite close to the adobe. I was concerned if the shaking continued, the pole would collapse on the building and us. At the same time, the carport to the right of us collapsed, just a few yards from where David and I were standing. But that was a small thing compared to watching the south end wall collapse.

Jeremy Fusco, the little boy from across the street, came running to us because his parents were gone and he was scared. He found us and we three went
out in the field behind the adobe and just stood there. We were cowering, wondering what was going to happen next, and suddenly a PG&E truck came roaring up Old Adobe Road. It stopped, and one of the crew looked at the power pole, and then ran over to look at the gas main nearby, and I yelled, "Stop! What's happening? Help—help, what's going on?" They replied, "We don't have time, we have to check all these power poles," and they went racing away.

Owner Edna Kimbro hopes the building can be repaired. "They're just not making them like that anymore." Courtesy of Kimbro Collection.

Not long after, my husband Joe came but he didn't see us in the back field. He was so upset he went through the entire house thinking we had been crushed inside! Joe crossed the kitchen where if David had stayed inside at the counter he would have been seriously hurt because all the kitchen cabinets fell onto the counters and floor. Everything came out and there was six inches of debris. Every glass, every dish, everything tumbled out and it all broke. Joe picked around down there, and then he went upstairs to my office and saw that everything up there had come crashing down as well. He was looking for our son in the debris. Finally he realized we were not in the house and came out and started yelling our names as he found us in the field.

One of us had to get our other son, Joey, in Watsonville, and as I was not in very good shape to do that, my husband went to Mintie White School. The teachers and the children were crying and huddled in a little

Edna Kimbro sitting at the back of her new home, the Castro Adobe. She had already brgun her fight to preserve the Castro Adobe. Courtesy of Kimbro Collection.

heap in the middle of the playing field, surrounded by downed power poles and lines crackling and crisping. Joe says there were things all over the road—it was a nightmare! David, Jeremy and I stayed in the field while Joe was gone.

Very soon many friends came to see what had happened because they were concerned about the adobe. Mary Ellen Irons and her husband Ben came and brought their big hefty son. She wasn't afraid to go inside and she pulled out food and tried to get things in order. We gathered blankets and bedding, and every minute we were in there, we worried that another quake would finish off the adobe and us.

We have a Volkswagen camper that I cannot bear to get rid of because I am sentimental about it (fortunately it was not in the carport). We grabbed a few things and the four of us slept in the camper. During the night there were aftershocks and the camper kept shaking back and forth. We didn't sleep, just lay there worrying. I was concerned that everything would go, as nothing of sentimental value had been retrieved.

The next morning we literally took a snow shovel we happened to have to get into the kitchen. The food was ruined. No one could phone us and we could not phone out. People just arrived; every night someone brought food. There were certain things in the *cocina* that were protected because of David Potter's heavy worktable. The whole house could have fallen on that table and it would have withstood it. So Joe went in and got all of our fancy wines, which happened to be stored under the worktable, and that morning we drank first-growth Bordeaux. We felt, "Why not? What does it all matter? This is what we have to drink—no milk." We were totally dependent on what people brought us. We did go into the *cocina* because the toilet and basin were still functioning. The plumbing was okay as it turned out, but we were afraid to go into the main house to use the facilities there or to stay in for any length of time. Friends brought us hard hats, and when we went in we wore them, and never went in alone. We slept in the Volkswagen for a week.

There was quite an adjustment for the Kimbro family to be made in the coming weeks-months-years. A friend in Shingle Springs was willing to loan them a trailer but it took some time to get it in shape to just travel and towed down to the adobe. It was a little twenty four foot trailer, but better than the Volkswagen van. In the interim their boys stayed with their grandparents until the trailer was moved and established. The adobe had been red tagged and deemed unsafe to move back into, so the condition of family's future was unknown. They lived in the little trailer three and a half months. The boys only got baths once a week when they went to Santa Cruz where Joe had an office at the Sash Mill with a kitchen bathroom, and futon bed. So, on weekends they stayed there. Weekends were lovely, but then they had to come back to the trailer and endure.

Soon however they read in the paper that FEMA was going to bring in these big trailers for people to live in who had lost their homes, but they were to be set up in a large parking lot in nearby Freedom and if they got one, they would have to live there. But eventually it was decided that FEMA would move the trailer out to the adobe site if fees were paid for moving and utility hook-up, which they did. Actually there were three off-site trailers in the county. Here, for three and one-half years the Kimbros lived in this six hundred and fifty square foot trailer, when eventually FEMA sent somebody for the trailer and it was returned to Texas.

It was a gradual realization that moving back into the adobe just wasn't going to work, because it would have personally cost far too much to bring it back to a safe living condition and there were other problems as well. Neither the state nor federal government wanted to loan for its renovation. Then it became an issue of fighting—not to move back into the adobe, but to keep it from being torn down! Edna realized that it was one thing that they were not going to move back there, but another to realize it may not survive at all! During this time the Kimbros were building a beautiful home on their property near the adobe, Edna continued her fight to save the adobe.

Edna Kimbro certainly was just the right person to commandeer such a fight. She is a renowned architectural conservator and historian, specializing in the research and preservation of Spanish and Mexican colonial architecture and the material culture of early California. She was an authority on the preservation of historic adobe structures who was instrumental in restoring a number of landmark buildings in California and who advocated new, less invasive techniques for conserving earthen architecture. Her frustration is understandable: As a member of the Getty Conservation Institute's Seismic Adobe Project, Kimbro helped document the destruction at adobes throughout Southern California. She was part of a team of earthen-architecture experts assembled by the institute, a research arm of the private, nonprofit J. Paul Getty Trust. Many of the buildings she surveyed remain badly damaged by quakes, but there are now signs of revival at three historically important adobes. She once said that quakes tend to wake people up to the value of these buildings. She wondered how many adobes we have to lose before we start preventing damage. During the 1980s she was involved in the restoration of the Santa Cruz Mission Adobe for California State Parks. As a stated historian for the California State Parks system, she aided in the preservation of numerous adobe structures in Central California.

Kimbro received a bachelor's degree in art history from the University of California, Santa Cruz. She studied seismic protection of historic adobe buildings in Rome. In 2003 she received the Norman Neuerburg Award from the California Mission Studies Association in recognition of her role as an advocate for the preservation and interpretation of California's mission past. She has devoted incredible amounts of time and energy to raising public awareness of the many threats to the survival of the remnants of California's Hispanic past, and to devising real-world solutions to address those threats. Edna also has a wealth of knowledge of a great number of California adobes reflected in many historic structure reports and similar documents she has authored over the years. Of particular importance to California are her contributions to the engineering solutions for seismic stabilization of historic adobe structures. It was well known in Watsonville that Edna Kimbro was fighting to preserve the Castro Adobe—she was on a mission. On Sunday, October 4, 1998, the *Sentinel* newspaper of Santa Cruz came out with an article,—*On a Mission*--by staff writer, Karen Clark, now a collection of the Castro Adobe Archives. It is quoted below, which goes into detail of the battle Edna Kimbro was up against:

> WATSONVILLE—One of the state's remaining two-story ranch-style adobes is in danger of crumbling after nine years of bureaucratic indifference. The Rancho San Andrés Castro Adobe, a state and national landmark on Old Adobe Road about 4 and one-half miles northwest of downtown Watsonville, was badly damaged in the Oct. 17, 1989, earthquake. Since then, owner Edna Kimbro, a nationally known adobe preservation expert, has been struggling without success to find a way to restore Pajaro Valley's first-ever state historic landmark and open it to the public.
>
> The irony isn't lost on Kimbro. "I can't do anything for the adobe but baby-sit it" Kimbro said. "It is ironic, and it's painful. But I can't squeeze blood from a turnip." The problem, of course, is money, and, according to some Pajaro Valley historians, a lack of interest from the county seat about all things south of Aptos.
>
> "Historically, Watsonville is that farming community in the south…and they don't want to relate to that," said Carolyn Swift, a Pajaro Valley native who is a member of the county's Historic Preservation Commission. "People in Watsonville have a hard time being taken seriously."
>
> Not so, said Assemblyman Fred Keeley, D-Boulder Creek, who was on the county Board of Supervisors during the years Kimbro tried to interest the county in repairing the adobe for public use. "I care about it." Said Keeley, who recently spent half a day at the Castro Adobe discussing how the state might play a role in repairing the 152- year-old structure. "I'm very interested in that issue. The adobe is a wonderful community

resource and state historic treasure." Keeley said generating local support is key to shaping a state budget strategy to buy and restore the adobe.

That's exactly what Kimbro has done over the past three months. With the help of longtime friend Charlene Duval—who years ago help save the historic Scott House in Scott's Valley—Kimbro has formed the ad hoc Committee to Save the Castro Adobe. The idea was Duval's, who returned to the area in time to revive Kimbro's flagging sprits after years of disappointments.

"She was fealing obviously down and battered and beaten down without heart," Duval said. "Our goal now is to have it open to the public for educational purposes, whoever buys it." The first step, said Kimbro, is to find about $15,000 to pay for a feasibility study that would satisfy county planners. Kimbro said county staff doesn't want to commit to a possible plan for the adobe without having an official proposal in hand. But Kimbro said she simply doesn't have the money to develop a costly proposal and then hope it flies with the county. "Their style is to say, 'You hire someone to come up with a proposal and we'll have a dart board, and you throw the darts and we'll tell you if you hit the bulls-eye.'" Kimbro said. "If you don't hit it, you get another dart to try again. It's like playing darts blindfolded." On the other hand, said the planner, they can't' be expected to give even tentative support to a non-existent proposal.

The larger problem, preservationists said, is that although the county's General Plan calls for an emphasis on preserving historic structures, officials don't provide any financial incentive to property owners to do so. Kimbro points to the city of Monterey, where owners of historic buildings get numerous financial and zoning breaks to encourage them to restore and maintain the area's structural treasures. "In the city of Monterey, if you own an historic property, they're falling all over themselves to help you", Kimbro said.

As an example of Santa Cruz County's alleged indifference to helping preserve historic buildings, Kimbro pointed out that it took five years and four revisions to win approval to split the Kimbros' Old Adobe Road parcel. After getting opposing directives from county planners, Kimbro said, she finally succeeded in getting Supervisor Walt Symons— in whose district the adobe sits—to step in and cut the red tape. The lot split was necessary to make it possible for a public or non-profit agency to buy the adobe parcel and make the necessary repairs.

Symons said he wants to help the adobe committee find grant money to pay for the feasibility study. He's not optimistic; however, the money will come from the already cash-strapped county. "It's an historic, original adobe in the county," said Symons. "But there are realities we have to face." Doni Tunheim, a historic preservationist who splits her time between Santa Cruz and northern Sonoma County, was a member of the county's Historic Preservation Commission in the early 1990s. Tunheim, a personal friend of Kimbro, resigned in protest over the way the county handled the Castro Adobe case the first four years after the quake. "It comes down to no money and a lack of political will by the Board of Supervisors and the state bureaucracy," Tunheim said.

Times may be changing, though. Pat Manning, Symons' representative on the county Historic Preservation Commission and a driving force behind the restoration of Valencia Hall above Aptos, has taken an interest in the Castro Adobe. "There seems to be more interest out there in preservation now than in the past," said Manning. "I feel like the time has come for the adobe."

Jan Beautz, chairwoman of the county Board of Supervisors, said if the board wasn't interested in historic preservation it wouldn't have a commission devoted to that very thing. "I would be willing to look at creative ways to make it easier for private people to keep their historic structures," Beautz said. "Maybe we could look at the Castro Adobe again and find a way to try to preserve it." In 1993, however, county officials estimated it would cost $1 million to repair the adobe, build a parking lot and upgrade Old Adobe Road to the historic rancho. "That kind of money," Beautz said, "simply isn't in the county's budget."

In the early years after the 1989 earthquake, Kimbro had hoped to borrow the money to make repairs from federal and state disaster-relief agencies. But not only was the state unwilling to loan her the money, the state Department of Housing and Community Development ordered Kimbro to tear it down and rebuild. The theory was it would be less costly to use the same septic tank, water well, etc., than to start over elsewhere on the large parcel. "I said no," said Kimbro, who enlisted the help of the state Office of Historic Preservation in her successful effort to fight off a demolition order as a condition of accepting the disaster loan.

Kimbro bristles at the notion her efforts to find a public or nonprofit agency to buy the adobe is her way to make money on the structure to pay off the mortgage on her new Adobe Road home next door.

"We owned that adobe free and clear," Kimbro said. "If we had just sold it to one of the private individuals who wanted to tear it down or remove the second story, we wouldn't have been paying taxes on both properties all this time…"

Kimbro has helped preserve several California adobes, particularly in Southern California after the 1991 Northridge earthquake. She also used her own money to restore the historic Branciforte adobe in Santa Cruz when her family owned the building before moving to the larger Castro Adobe. But the Castro Adobe doesn't have the prominence among county residents that the Branciforte and Mission Hill adobes have generated over the years. "When I was growing up in Watsonville, I didn't even know it was there," Swift said. "I think it needs to be rediscovered." Kimbro said the adobe's profile is one reason it's threatened now. "The Castro Adobe is important because it demonstrates to people what the culture that came before us was capable of producing, and did produce," said Kimbro.

Historians believe Jose Joaquin Castro built the original one-story adobe in the 1830s after being chased away from his former rancho near the current KOA campground on San Andreas Road by American Indians who were there first. Castro, a member of the historic Juan Baptiste de Anza expedition was rewarded for his service to the crown in 1822 with the Rancho San Andrés land grant. Jose Joaquin Castro died in 1838, leaving it to his son, Juan Jose Castro, to enlarge the family's adobe to a two-story showpiece that rivaled anything in the showier town of Monterey.

"They are not real common," Kimbro said. "This is the only one built in this area. They were more common in Monterey, which is why that two-story style is named Monterey." At one point, the Castro family owned land grants ranging from the Pajaro River to Ano Nuevo. But eventually, they lost those holdings to American squatters who had the backing of American courts. The Castros also ran afoul of their neighbors, the Amestis, who waged a decades-long court battle in the late 1800s to win a land dispute. Despite their vast land holdings, the Castros always gathered at the adobe for parties, not only because of its size, but because it had the only fandango room in the county.

Castro descendants haven't lost track of their roots. On Oct. 11, the family plans to meet at Wilder Ranch (another of the family's former land holdings) to celebrate the 200th anniversary of their arrival in what is now California. A few plan to visit the adobe, one-time home to the family's patriarch. "I think it should be saved," said Charles Kieffer, a local business man and Castro descendent. "In Santa Cruz County there are only four adobes left of all the ones built during the Spanish era." Kieffer wonders if the tradition of early American settlers in California to wipe out evidence of Spanish and Mexican heritage might still be at work today in subtler ways. There seems to be less interest in Santa Cruz County to save its Spanish and Mexican heritage compared to Monterey," Kieffer said. "I think that heritage and history is involved with things you can see and touch and feel. This is actually a building they lived in. It just makes a connection."

Castro family historian Marion Pokriots plans to attend the reunion with a petition for family members to sign urging the restoration of the adobe. News of the reunion isn't the only thing preservationists hope will spark renewed interest in the Castro Adobe. In January, Watsonville City Councilman Tony Campos will take his place on the county Board of Supervisors. When he does, he will become only the second Latino in county history to hold that seat. The first, Juan Jose Castro—the architect of what now is such a rare two-story, rancho-style adobe—who joined the board in 1853.

"It's exciting at this particular moment in time...that the house that was the home of the first Mexican American member of the Board of Supervisors is at this point in its exciting evolution," said Diane Porter Cooley, a longtime advocate of preserving Pajaro Valley's history. "I think it's a very, very significant thing to recognize that we have a local Hispanic heritage."

So, from the *Sentinel's* article above of Santa Cruz, it can readily be seen that there was quite a struggle to save the Castro Adobe from destruction. It took not only the driving effort of Edna Kimbro, but numerous others to become interested to move forward the challenge to save the adobe. But things were now looking much better. Now, there seemed to be a light beaming at the end of the tunnel. The following Santa Cruz *Sentinel* article—*State Cash for Historic Adobe*—by staff writer Robin Musitelli, now in the collection of Charles Kieffer, presents good news about the interest and support from the state of California, with its intention of purchase and repair of the Rancho San Andrés Castro Adobe:

SACRAMENTO—Watsonville's only state historic landmark and the South County's only Spanish-heritage building will be kept from crumbling, thanks to a hefty appropriation in the state budget. The budget, as approved by the state Senate Tuesday, contains $950,000 to purchase and repair Rancho San Andrés Castro Adobe, a state and national landmark on Old Adobe Road northwest of Watsonville. The adobe is one of the state's few remaining two-story, ranch-style adobes. The 154-year-old building was damaged in the 1989 Loma Prieta earthquake, and damaged further in winter storms in 1995. It now is fenced off and in danger of collapsing. "If approved by the Assembly and Gov. Davis, the state allocation will purchase the old adobe and pay for some repairs," said Edna Kimbro, a nationally known adobe preservation expert who owns the adobe. "It won't completely restore it to how it was in 1846, but it will be useable and will put it back the way it was before the earthquake," she said.

The Kimbro family lived in the adobe before the earthquake crumbled one wall. The family was unable to secure federal or state money to rebuild, and used the adobe as collateral to build a new home nearby. Instead of selling to just anyone, Kimbro wanted to sell it to the state to have it preserved. She was initially rebuffed, so she and other adobe supporters turned to the county Board of Supervisors. When that effort failed, she once again turned to state officials, this time with very different results. "It's taken us 10 years to get here," she said Tuesday. Don't plan on a tour soon, however. Even if the money remains in the budget, there isn't enough to staff the adobe to open it to the public. Kimbro and an ad hoc committee are hoping to identify a nonprofit organization to run it for the state.

Historians believe Jose Joaquin Castro built the adobe, originally a one-story structure, in the 1830s after being chased away from his rancho near the current KOA Campground on San Andreas Road by American Indians. Castro, a member of the historic Juan Baptiste de Anza expedition from Sinaloa, Mexico to Monterey, was rewarded for the service to the crown in 1822 with a land grant. Jose Joaquin Castro died in 1838, leaving the adobe to his son, Juan Jose Castro, who enlarged the family home to a two-story showpiece that rivaled anything in Monterey. Juan Jose Castro was also the first Latino in the county history to be elected to the county Board of Supervisors.

"The Castro Adobe was the only two-story adobe built in this area," Kinbro said. It's also the only adobe remaining that "speaks directly to the Hispanic heritage of this area," she said. Kimbro said she hopes that ultimately the adobe will be restored to its 1946 splendor. "The state funding to get the building useable, safe and in public ownership is a first step, and a major first step," she said. "I'm just thrilled about this."

Things now began to look up for Edna Kimbro and the others who were working hard to save the Castro Adobe from destruction. Ben Angove, a county parks director said, "They're just not making them like that anymore." At this time the Castro Adobe was recently one of seven sites named a historical landmark, to the delight of Edna Kimbro, who believed that the award to the Castro Adobe would be very beneficial in later obtaining funding for its restoration. The following Santa Cruz *Sentinel* newspaper article—*Historical Status for Adobe*—in the Charles Kieffer Collection, written by staff writer Keith Muraoka, further praises the Castro Adobe status, now a California Landmark:

The restored Hansen house as viewed from Old Adobe Road. Photo courtesy of Wanda Morton.

WATSONVILLE—South County is now the proud owner of its first ever state historical landmark. The 145 year-old Castro Adobe, technically known as the Rancho San Andrés Castro Adobe, was one of seven sites named a historical landmark Friday by the State Historical Resourses Commission in Sacramento. The two-story, 3,800-square-foot Castro Adobe is located in the Calabasas area. It is privately owned by Edna Kimbro, an architectural conservator, who is well known in local historical circles.

Kimbro hopes that the state historical landmark designation may result in state monies to repair the adobe, which was heavily damaged in the October 1989 earthquake. Santa Cruz County Parks Director Ben Angove agreed that the state designation "strengthens our position" as to the possibilities of getting grants to repair the adobe. Much of the south wall of the adobe collapsed in the earthquake. There are deep cracks in the north wall and part of the original kitchen tottered over. The adobe has since been fenced off.

Kimbro, who had been living in the adobe, but now is living in a trailer on the site, said repair estimates vary widely—from $300,000 to $500,000. "Neither the Federal Emergency Management Agency or federal Small Business Administration will repair the historical building," Kimbro said. "Funds that are available to private homeowners will not cover this type of restoration, even though it was sustained in the earthquake," she said. Besides hoping the state may come to the rescue of the historical landmark, Kimbro has offered the adobe to the county for the price of the land alone. She has also been in contact with the state Parks Department. "I don't care who repairs it, as long as it gets repaired," Kimbro said. Her dream is to see the adobe restored and opened as a historic park, similar to Santa Cruz Mission. "It would be very important for the Pajaro Valley, considering 60 percent of the population is Hispanic," she said. "There's a crying need for a historic park in the Pajaro Valley.

"They're just not making them like that anymore," she said. "The county has already done a preliminary study on the adobe," Angove said. Purchase, renovation and repair of the adobe, as well as construction of a road and parking lot are estimated to cost $1 million. "Of course, the county—like other public agencies—simply doesn't have the money. We've got it on hold unless we can identify a funding source," Angove said.

The state historical landmark designation makes the Castro Adobe one of eight in Santa Cruz County. The others range from the Santa Cruz

Beach Boardwalk and Santa Cruz Mission to the Felton Covered Bridge. The adobe is one of only four California Rancho-era adobes in the county and, by far, the largest one. It was built in 1846 by the Castro family, who along with the Rodriguez family, where the two principal founders of the Pajaro Valley. At one point, the Castro family owned more than 11,000 acres from Aptos to Watsonville.

The dedication of the bronze California Landmark #998 was an exciting event in the gardens on October 17, 2000, with the plaque itself, financed by the Pajaro Valley Historical Association. Fred Keeley, speaker Pro Tem of the California State Assembly, who carried the legislation to make the Rancho San Andrés Castro Adobe a State Historic Park, was the primary speaker at the ceremony. The article below—*Officials to Honor Historic Adobe*—in the Santa Cruz *Sentinel* by Ester Rodriguez brings us one step closer to the Castro Adobe site actually becoming a state park:

> One of the counties' last surviving historical adobes, which was in danger of being torn down after sustaining extensive damage in the Loma Prieta earthquake 11 years ago, appears ready for a new life. State and county officials at 10 a.m. today, will mark the anniversary of the 1989 quake by unveiling a state historical-land mark plaque at the San Andrés Castro Adobe. That signals that a deal with the state to repair and restore the historic building may soon be signed.
>
> The 3,800-square-foot adobe, made out of sun-dried mud bricks is the largest and only two-story historical hacienda in the county. The hacienda is one of the first examples of Monterey-style architecture, which is a national style that developed out of Monterey. "The building has basically risen from its embers," said Edna Kimbro, a historical-preservation expert who owns the adobe. Construction on the building began in 1846.
>
> A year ago, Gov. Gray Davis approved a budget request by Assemblyman Fred Keeley, D-Boulder Creek, for $950,000 in state money to buy and repair the adobe. Since then, Kimbro and the state have been negotiating on a purchase price and exactly what repairs will be done. "The Spanish-style hacienda is the only state-and nationally recognized historical building in Watsonville. It is one of 350 adobes and missions that have survived in the state," Kimbro said. "In its time, this was a happening social place and political matters were made here," said David

Vincent, superintendent of the state Parks Department's Santa Cruz district, which will supervise public access to the building once the deal is finalized. "The adobe is important to California's cultural heritage," he said.

When the deal is finalized, the adobe, and the Old Adobe Road in Watsonville, will be the third state-operated adobes in the county, after the Santa Cruz Mission, on Mission Hill, and the Bolcoff Adobe at Wilder Ranch State Park. The adobe was badly damaged in the quake with collapsed and cracked walls. "Since then, only minor repairs have been done," said Kimbro, who was living in the building at the time of the earthquake.

Vincent said negations could take up to six months, but added that once the parks department takes over the building repair plans will be drawn up. Road improvements also are planned. Retrofitting will involve removing part of the roof and securing it with steel anchors. "That way, if there were another earthquake, the walls would not collapse," Kimbro said. The renovation process should take about three years. Throughout the life of the old adobe, it has primarily been used as a residence except when it was abandoned in 1906 and used as a barn and apricot shed. The building was built by some of the first Spanish settlers to California, who arrived in 1776. Local historians believe one of the members, Jose Joaquin Castro, of the historical Juan Baptista de Anza expedition from Mexico built the home.

NINE

The year 2002 was an exciting time for many persons acquainted with the Castro Adobe, the year that it was eyed for as a California State Park; there was a celebration in honor of this event. The author and his wife Margaret attended the celebration at the Castro Adobe for this event, at which time Assemblyman Fred Keeley encouragingly spoke to the group assembled in the Castro Adobe gardens including: families who had acted as stewards of the historic treasure, numerous Castro descendants of the original Castro family, and interested persons in general. It was extremely reminiscent to the author, having lived next to this great Castro Adobe structure over a half century ago. He was so happy to hear that it was now going to be taken over by the state and renovated. However, there were hurdles to be met and it was soon learned the process would take some years.

Volunteers from left to right: Charlie Kieffer, Jim Brownson, Jim Toney, Jessica Kurz, and Barney Levy (Randy Widers not pictured). Friends of Santa Cruz State Parks photo.

It was at this time that he personally met Suzanne Paizis and Edna Kimbro. He had corresponded with Suzanne during her writing of her book, *The Joaquin Castro Adobe in the Twentieth Century*, given her an interview of his early years there and presented for inclusion in her book a section entitled, *Remembrances of the Castro Adobe*. It was such a great pleasure for him meeting these two ladies who had done so much to promote an endurance of the Castro Adobe, a structure throughout the years that had become so entwined in his life. It certainly was a grand event and meeting so many people directly related to the old Castro Adobe was quite inspiring to him.

Volunteers pouring adobe into the brick forms on the grounds of the Castro Adobe. After the bricks are dried they are removed and stored. Friends of Santa Cruz States Parks photo.

It was thought at this time by many the state of California would directly and quickly take over the reins and quickly make the Castro Adobe a full-supported state park. However, this has not been the case, and even today, some six or so years later, the Castro Adobe has not yet received full state park status. On the other hand, Friends of Santa Cruz State Parks, who have been stewarding State Parks in Santa Cruz County since 1976, have stepped in to help restore the Castro Adobe; albeit, with the help of many volunteers. A recent article by Jessica Kusz, *Saving the Castro Adobe, One Brick at a Time*, is a story of the initial endeavor to prepare enough adobe bricks to complete the renovation of the adobe walls. The article follows below along with pictures from the blog of Friends of Santa Cruz State Parks:

Inspecti prepared on of adobe blocks. Courtesy of Friends of Santa Cruz State Parks

"One brick at a time" certainly was the process for saving the Rancho San Andrés Castro Adobe as volunteers endured heavy lifting, wheel barrowing, dirt sifting, and punching mud into wood molds to hand make the vital adobe bricks. The Castro Adobe was built in 1848-1849 by Juan Jose Castro, son of Jose Joaquin Castro (an original De Anza party member). It is the largest two-story adobe rancho building constructed in the Monterey Bay Region, containing the only fandango room outside of Monterey. Purchased by adobe conservationist, Edna Kimbro and her husband Joe in 1988, it was severely damaged in the 1989 earthquake and was purchased by the California State Parks in 2002. The authentic early-California building and its setting possess tremendous potential for interpretation of the rural lifestyle and culture of Mexican California.

The large supply of bricks are all covered awaiting use in the construction of damaged walls of the Castro Adobe, especially the south wall that fell down during the Loma Prieta earthquake. Friends of Santa Cruz State Parks photo.

The production of the bricks was an essential step in stabilizing the building for future interpretation. Guided by Tim Aguilar, expert adobe brick maker, and Friends of Santa Cruz State Parks (FSCSP) and board and staff, and over 150 volunteers were able to make 2,500 bricks in July and August 2007. It was truly remarkable to see the dedication of volunteers and board members who joined together to produce the adobe

New stones that were intregrated to maintain the appearance of the original construction of the adobel foundation of the cocina. Friends of Santa Cruz State Parks photo.

bricks on site. Although the brick making project was fairly streamlined by the time the volunteers arrived, it was a bumpy road to finding the right components for the project. Who would think finding the right dirt would be such a dilemma? It was. Jim Toney, FSCSP board member and Jessica Kusz, Staff Project Manager, spent much time searching and testing to find the perfect dirt composition and compression.

Ultimately, the best dirt for the project was from a local source, Central Home Supply. Owner of Central Home Supply, Rick Santee, was extremely helpful and provided much assistance in procuring and delivering the right dirt for the project. After receiving a front-page article in the *Register Pajaronian* which interviewed Castro descendant, Charlie Kiefer, the volunteer applications flooded into the Friends' office. We were amazed at the number of interested community members who wanted to work. Now, we had our volunteers and the site had to be readied for the work to begin.

The Friends staff and board provided their help with clean-up and set up for the first day. Joe Kimbro was kind enough to allow us to use his land for making and drying of the bricks and served as our unofficial brick guardian, making sure the bricks were safeguarded during curing. The staff and board cleared the site, sifted dirt, readied the molds and even made a few bricks to jump start the project. On July 27th the first 40 yards of dirt was dumped at the site and the first batch of volunteers arrived on Saturday, July 28th, ready to work. After a brief orientation, the volunteers were off and making bricks. Board members helped keep things running smoothly. Barney Levy, jack of all trades, managed to sift dirt, run the mixer, dump mixed dirt into wheelbarrows, wheelbarrow dirt to the molds, and still keep a smile on his face. We had to order him to take breaks!

Tim Aguilar bounced from each work station imparting his expertise to each volunteer. Jim Brownson and Jim Toney utilized their management skills to keep everything running like clockwork while also sifting dirt and making bricks. Board members Lani LeBlanc and Linda Hoff greeted volunteers, delivered a delicious lunch, and worked making bricks too. Charlie Kiefer kept everyone entertained during lunch by giving a talk on the history of the Castro Adobe. If volunteers were unable to do heavy lifting, then they were assigned to covering the bricks with large pieces of paper and watering the bricks. To prevent cracking, the bricks had to be watered approximately three times a day for seven days to keep them fairly damp during the slow drying process. Thankfully, a close neighbor, Cathy Rose, was able to help us by watering in the early morning and early evening. Our first volunteer day we made 250 bricks! It was an incredible start to a truly outstanding project.

The start of laying adobe bricks at the north wall of the cocina. Friends of Santa Cruz State Parks photo.

In between the volunteer days, the California Conservation Corps (CCC), worked on the project and bricks and provided outstanding service to the Castro Adobe. Organized by Brenda Herrmann and supervised by crew chief, Sharon Hazel, the CCC crew was instrumental in the creation of over half the bricks needed for the project. They learned the art of brick making and also got to know certain board members who volunteered during the week. Lani was a big hit with the CCC and she had them convinced that she had worked as a drill sergeant in the past and we are still researching that one and have neither been able to confirm or deny.

The following two Saturdays were also volunteer days, August 4th and August 11th. The work moved along smoothly and they were able to make approximately 500 bricks total on both days. Once the bricks were stable, they were stood on their side to cure completely. The bricks were quite large, 14 inches by 28 inches and weighing over 75 pounds! The CCC and FSCSP board members had the difficult job of standing the 2,500 bricks for drying. Although it was hard work, the visual of so many bricks standing, waiting to be utilized made the team members proud.

In total, the project took just over three weeks to make 2,500 bricks with less than 14% breakage. With the help of Tim Aguilar, volunteers, business members, Friends of Santa Cruz State Parks board and staff, the Castro Adobe will be saved! Edna Kimbro, the founding catalyst behind the preservation of the Castro Adobe passed away in 2005, and Friends of the Santa Cruz State Parks is pleased to continue her mission. We are currently in the process of loading the bricks onto pallets to be stored for later use. The California State Parks is charged with maintaining, restoring, and stabilizing the historic building. They will utilize the bricks in the stabilization of the historic adobe and the bricks sit on pallets awaiting their final destination! We hope that all the hard work has paid off and that work on the building can begin as soon as possible.

It is observed from the above article that in mid-2007 an extensive effort had been made to make enough adobe bricks needed for restoring the Castro

Cracks like these were found in certain areas of the Castro Adobe walls and needed to be filled. Friends of Santa Cruz State Park photo.

Adobe walls. Now on Wednesday, November 28, 2007, Friends of Santa Cruz State Parks supplied their first post to the Castro Adobe blog—*Chronicling the Castro Adobe*. They were much excited to be able to chronicle the ongoing efforts to stabilize and restore the Castro Adobe. They noted that they hoped this can be a place to share ideas, history, upcoming opportunities or anything else related to this incredible building. They are sure it will also be exciting to the reader to follow along the chronicle pathway during the restoration of the adobe that is to follow.

Pancho Villa is filling a crack of one of the Castro Adobe walls. After this job is finished, then the wall has to be sanded and leveled and then white washed. Friends of Santa Cruz State Parks photo.

Late in the year, Wednesday, December 5, 2007, a group went out to the Adobe to inspect how secure it was for the upcoming winter. From the inspection it was decided that new tarps were needed on the roof to protect the building from the upcoming rainy season. They were later installed by the State maintenance crew; this should keep most of the weather out for the season. The new adobe bricks that were previously covered were now to be checked to ensure that they were staying dry.

Upon inspection the next day it was found that the method of covering with thick plastic seemed to be working well and that water had been diverted. However, fallen leaves were brushed off the tops of the bricks so that water would not collect on top. A few pinhole openings in the pallet covers were patched with duct tape. It was found that some of the rubber bands snapped which bound the top of the pallet covers; they evidently were very susceptible to UV. The rubber bands were replaced with twine. Other than that, the adobe bricks seemed to be doing well.

Each volunteer was given the oportunity to lay one adobe brick in the cocina wall and each happily did so. Friends of Santa Cruz State Parks photo.

On Wednesday, January 2, 2008, a small group of workers ventured out to the Castro Adobe to do a primary check of adobe bricks to see how they were fairing through the winter. Their main concern was water wicking up from the ground and penetrating the bricks as well as water pooled on top of the bricks infiltrating the pallet covers. They uncovered a sampling of bricks and found that their method of covering them with plastic pallet covers was mostly working to keep the brick dry! The overall condition of the bricks was excellent, with only a few displaying a small amount of moisture condensation on the tops of the bricks.

The east wall of the cocina is shown under construction and the new rafters are in place on the roof. Friends of Santa Cruz State Parks photo.

One brick had some wicking at the bottom and was soft enough that with a strong force (Randy's thumb) an indentation was made into the brick. That condition appeared on one brick and overall the base of the bricks appeared to be withstanding the rain and moisture well. One issue they noted was that the large rubber bands used to secure the tops of the pallet covers were snapping due to UV exposure. The bands that had broken were replaced with twine and thus the twine vs. rubber bands experiment was answered. For use outdoors, twine was found to endure much better than the large rubber bands. A big storm was predicted to be approaching tomorrow; and their next step was to clear away any branches that had fallen on or near the bricks before they finished the day's work.

They also planned later to clear the weeds growing around the base of the pallets. If this were done, then assurance would be expected that the bricks would be protected for the remaining winter months.

After the bricks were completed on the south gable wall they were whitewshed to protect them from rain and moisture. Friends of Santa Cruz State Parks photo.

So on Wednesday, January 16, a few of the work party ventured out into the cold Central California winter to do some upkeep on the bricks and perform weed control around each pallet. The first job was to clear the quickly growing weeds surrounding the pallets. They also attempted to clear the dirt underneath the pallets (pushed up underneath by gophers) to ensure a steady air flow from the ground to the bricks. They took the covers off a few sample pallets to check the condition of the bricks. Most of them appeared in good condition although some had suffered a bit of water damage, generally due to covers shifting in the recent storms and exposing portions of the bricks. Some bricks exhibited moisture from condensation, although this is a fairly common occurrence when bricks are covered and stored. They noted that dirt piled up underneath the bricks did not appear to be causing the expected damage to the bottom of the bricks...of course they didn't discover this until after they had cleaned out most of the dirt. In one instance, the plastic cover had blown off half of the pallet which exposed a portion of the bricks to the elements. Up until this point, it has been demonstrated much work was not only involved in manufacturing the bricks, but in maintaining them in good condition to be used in forthcoming adobe wall construction.

This is a view of the new rafters that were installed on the Castro Adobe roof. Note the stainless steel bars at upper right that were put in the adobe brick walls. Courtesy of Friends of Santa Cruz

But on Tuesday, February 21st, the lingering time had arrived and work had now begun on the Castro Adobe! The long awaited seismic stabilization was underway. The work began with a group of California Conservation Corps (CCC) members and Direct Construction Unit (DCU) crew setting up scaffolding for the project. The DCU foreman, Chris Barrazza and his crew moved quickly.

The interior of the *cocina* (historic kitchen) wall with gable end was dismantled and CCC members carefully removed the historic corner shelves from the *cocina* wall and dismantled the fireplace as well as other non-historic interior

The roof over the veranda was raised 13 inches so that there was plenty of head room while walking under them on the veranda. Friends of Santa Cruz State Parks photo.

features of the building. Part of the south gable wall was exposed and was assessed for the best way possible to maintain the original adobe bricks so they might integrate them with the new adobe bricks made in summer of 2007.

At this point, the state archaeologist, Karen Hildebrand was rapidly finishing her documentation of the *cocina* wall before the DCU crew dismantled the damaged wall. Volunteers from the Santa Cruz Archaeological Society assisted Karen by removing the plaster from the interior north wall. Karen was excited to locate the original vent holes, and view smoke stains and holes for cooking tools in the *cocina* wall. Locating these will ensure the correct placement of the *bracero* (masonry range) in the interpretive plan in the future.

On March 3-5th, 2008, work continued on the north cocina wall. As the wall was dismantled, the river cobblestone foundation was exposed. Archaeologist Karen Hildebrand explained that the foundation appeared to consist of various layers of courses of river cobblestone throughout the north wall. The west end of the foundation was composed of cobblestone which were two layers thick and three courses across. The east end was similar in layers yet but only consisted of two courses at the perimeter of the base. This type of foundation was quite different from the rest of the building.

After the cobblestone was recorded through photographs and detailed drawings, the stones were removed and a 30-inch trench was dug to accommodate the new foundation of concrete and rebar. The new foundation will not be visible in the reconstruction and the existing river cobblestone will be integrated to maintain the appearance of the original construction. March 3 work continued to uncover the many layers of history and the project archaeologist Karen Hildebrand was on hand so that each layer was understood and captured. Here it was noticed that earthquakes have forever been a nemesis to the adobe.

Work for the week of March 10-14th focused mostly on repair of the south gable end wall of the adobe. The wall had partially collapsed in the 1989 Loma Prieta earthquake. The DCU crew removed the adobe brick until a sound surface was located. After preparation for the new foundation, concrete was pumped in on Monday March 17.

A day later the original cobblestone rocks were inserted back into the new concrete foundation to maintain the appearance of the original foundation wall. Here is where they began the difficult task of rebuilding the adobe wall with new bricks (made on site last summer by dedicate volunteers and CCC staff!) Work on the wall continued this week which included laying the bricks, pouring the mud mortar by DUC crew at each new level, and spreading the mortar before placement of new brick layers. The placing of the approximately 85 pound bricks into place was quite a task. The week of March 17-20 work continued on repair of the south gable end-wall. Reconstruction of the corners of the adobe building can be the most technical and time consuming as the new adobe bricks must be 'stitched in' with the existing adobe bricks. Other on going work this week included the reconstruction of the *cocina* foundation wall. The rebar cage was constructed and installed into the deep hole which will become the base of the cocina wall.

The week of March 24-28 work focused on the completion of the south gable wall. More of the cobblestones were installed at the foundation base and a few of the adobe brick courses were completed. Also this week, construction began on the east *cocina* wall at the doorway. Bruce Ihle and the CCC crew carefully cut the bricks while Poncho Villa laid the bricks in courses, halfway completing by weeks end.

On Wednesday, April 2, 2008, over 20 volunteers from the summer 2007 brick making project were given a great opportunity to be able to lay one of the bricks in the north *cocina* wall. The adobe bricks laid in the wall were the bricks volunteers had made in July and August 2007. Along with the assistance of the DCU and the CCC crew, the volunteers were able to spread the mortar and help set the brick in place. Both the *Santa Cruz Sentinel* and the *Register-Pajaronian* were on site to document the incredible event.

The week of April 7-11 work focused on the *cocina* walls. Most of the work was concentrated on the north *cocina* wall. Last week the first courses of the wall were laid by brick making volunteers from last summer. Later, the DCU and CCC crews continued work on the wall. The coming week work was expected to be completed on the north wall. On the interior of the *cocina* wall, the original shelves were incorporated with the new adobe wall. The doorway which led from the *cocina* to the modern kitchen was filled-in. Historically, there had been no door from the interior of the *cocina* to the new building; this door was cut through the wall by a recent past resident of the adobe. The east wall where the bathroom in the *cocina* was previously located was completed and by April the north *cocina* wall was almost complete, including the historic opening to allow smoke from the *bracero* to escape.

Meanwhile, the DCU and CCC crew had been working on the top gable end of the south wall. The gable end was at the top of the south end of the building and therefore the scaffolding for the project was a serious feat. A large ladder leads to the top of the scaffolding where the work was taking place. During this time the exterior walls were also undergoing crack repair. The cracks were first scraped to remove loose mud and plaster. After they had been scraped and vacuumed, DCU crew member, Bruce Ihle, sprayed water and wet the cracks. He then used a grout bag to inject mud into the cracks. DCU crew member, Pancho Villa, then coated and scored the mud plaster over the cracks. It was then let to dry for 3-4 days.

During May 15-30 more crack repair was continued on other adobe walls. The west wall underwent quite a bit of repair. Pancho Villa removed unstable adobe and cleaned out between the bricks and mortar on this wall. After the wall was cleaned, new bricks were inserted in between the courses along with new mortar. The final result after the new bricks and mortar had been inserted is to plaster the wall, the final step before the wall is whitewashed.

During the above interval, on May 20 core drilling began. Work started on the new *cocina* walls and has now moved to the east wall of the adobe building. Nichols Concrete Cutting is a company that specializes, among other things, in core drilling. Having much experience in drilling adobe walls, Nichols' work moved along nicely. The process includes a hole which is drilled through the adobe walls and a stainless steel rod is then inserted into each hole. The hole and rod run the vertical height of the wall. The rods are spaced roughly 1 and 1/2 feet apart and filled with epoxy. This will make the structure much more stable in a seismic event.

During the period of June 2-6 core drilling was almost completed. Nichols Concrete Cutting moved very quickly with two crews of four and work was essentially finished within the above dates. The core drilling was a fascinating process to follow. The first task is actually drilling the hole for the stainless steel rods. The crew had to wear a fairly substantial mask due to the dust. While the crew is working on the top of the roof, another crew member drills two small holes, one about 2/3 way down the wall and another about 3 feet from the bottom of the wall. These two holes are used to relieve pressure as the drill comes down creating the hole. The dirt and dust that is created in the drilling process needs to be allowed to escapes and these holes allow that to happen. The end result of the dirt/dust blasting out of the hole is remarkable. Not only does quite a bit blast out of the hole, but it comes out fast. Once the hole is complete it was vacuumed out and the stainless steel rod was inserted and later void around it filled with epoxy.

During June 9-13, the DCU construction crew completed the mud plastering of the interior of the new *cocina* wall, with the corner shelves anchored to the new wall to the left and the original wall to the right. Also completed was the scratch coat of the mud plaster on the exterior of the *cocina* walls. Then a smooth plaster coat which looked similar to the interior *cocina* walls was applied.

The lintels (Wood support members above a door or window) above the windows and doors were repaired. A few of the lintels were damaged and wood members were replaced and/or repaired with epoxy, then plastered over to match the existing plaster. With the core drilling complete, work shifted toward the roof. The CCC crew began removing the roof sheathing to prepare the area for construction of the new roof, which was scheduled to begin in a week.

These signs were placed on the fence at the bottom of Old Adobe Road leading to the Castro Adobe soon after the Trabing fire. Local residents wished to express their thanks to firemen for controlling the fire. Friends of Santa Cruz State Parks photo.

The Trabing Fire that burned through the area and next to the Castro Adobe State Historic Park on former Rancho San Andrés in June 20 was frightening to Friends of Santa Cruz State Parks, as well as many other property owners in its path. Thanks to the efforts of Cal Fire firefighters, the fire was held to grass areas near the two-story Monterey-Colonel-style structure. "We were thrilled with this news and incredibly grateful for the efforts made by Cal Fire firefighters," said Randy Widera, director of strategic development and partnerships for Friends of Santa Cruz State Park. Watching the fire unfold was terrifying and if there is one things that FSCSP, DCU crew, and State parks has learned—it is that they are all very dedicated to the Castro Adobe! That was evident from all the frantic phone calls, e-mails, etc. As they launched into the 'Save the Castro Adobe' campaign that summer this fire so clearly illustrated the importance of saving the Castro Adobe. Not only is it an incredible historic resource today but the thought of its destruction mobilized so many people, proving how vital it is to our future.

Chris Barraza had left for the weekend on Friday to his home 5 hours away. Once hearing of the fire he promptly packed his things back up and made the trek back up to the Castro Adobe on Saturday. He was not going to sit by while a fire (potentially) burned the Castro Adobe! Somehow he talked his way up Old Adobe Road and onto the property and proceeded to protect the building, help neighbors, and even gave water to the neighbor's thirsty goats. It was obvious that they were very lucky. Chris had stated that while he was driving out to the Castro Adobe to see the damage from the Trabing Fire, that when driving into the intersection of Larkin Valley Road and Buena Vista Road it was heart wrenching…seeing all the burned trees and dark pastures combined with the smell of smoke was difficult. However, when he got to the intersection of Old Adobe Road it was wonderful to see the tribute and thanks to the firefighters.

The DCU crew and the CCC crew had cut down a lot of the grass, keeping it short, so the fire really had no fuel to burn. Chris Barraza (DCU foreman) said that a neighbor had put out the three spot fires and they never spread to other areas on the property.

Thankfully, most of Old Adobe Road area was not damaged. Some of the homes on the west side of the street had fire reach to their decks, but the houses were intact. As we know, other houses on Larkin Valley Road and Trabing Road were not as lucky. At the Castro Adobe, there was evidence of at least three spot fires, one which burned a small wood shed covering a pump, one at the entrance to Joe Kimbro's property, and one spot fire which burned a pallet of the adobe bricks and melted the plastic on another.

During July 7-11 the roof for the *cocina* was in the midst of construction with twenty redwood rafters, dimension of 3 by 6 inches times 16 feet long. The rafters were connected to the brackets which were welded to the steel plate, a plate that was anchored to the stainless steel rods in the adobe walls. After completion of this roof, construction was scheduled to begin on the main roof.

During July 14-18 construction on the main roof of the adobe was in progress. New wood rafters were installed on the roof framing. Most of the original wood rafters were allowed to stay in place but the new rafters were added which worked in conjunction with the new steel rods and metal plates in the adobe walls. Bruce Ihle installed some of the new rafters and the DCU crew also worked in hand on the roof with the new and old wood framing, putting the new wood framing in place. On the second floor, only the minimum amount of the ceiling was removed in order to protect the interior portions of the building. Only a few feet of the interior ceiling had to be removed and exposed.

On July 21-25 roof construction continued both on the *cocina* and main roof. Roof work on the *cocina* included the installation of the redwood sheeting which was placed on the rafters. The roof on the *cocina* essentially consisted of two roof coverings which created an accurate historical representation of the roof from interior and from exterior. From the interior of the *cocina*, one now sees exposed cedar shingles which were originally visible from inside the room of the *cocina*. These were topped by painted black plywood sheathing and then barn shingles were installed on the exterior of the *cocina* roof. At this juncture, rafters continued to be installed on the main house. The roof on the balcony on the east side of the building was also reconstructed. Due to various renovations to the exterior, the pitch of the original balcony was altered and was too low. Therefore, the balcony roof was raised in conjunction with the new roof on the main house.

Although it was exciting to see the new shingles finished on the *cocina* during July 28-31, it was even more gratifying to see the lime wash which was being applied to the exterior of the building. The repaired cracks got a coat of mud plaster, then a coat of lime wash. Another two coats of lime wash was applied over the entire surface. The new wall of the *cocina* got three coats of lime wash. On the main roof all the seventy 3 inch times 8 inch rafter installations were near completion. Each rafter was braced by structural steel to further reinforce the rafter and was bolted to the stainless steel rods which were drilled earlier into the adobe walls.

On August 11-14 lime whitewashing moved to the east lower side of the building. Pancho Villa was first seen here painting on the thin lime wash. There followed approximately 3-4 coats applied to this exterior wall to complete the process. This wall matched the extraordinary results as seen on the west side of the building. At this point, the cracks in the upper east wall in the balcony were repaired as well, and will receive the lime wash next. The new adobe bricks installed on the south gable end wall had been completely covered with lime wash by this time.

During August 25-28 a crane was use to lift the very heavy stainless pieces into place on the roof. First though, DCU foreman Chris Barazza had to have the stainless steel pieces cinched down to be lifted onto the roof. These pieces were placed along the rake (top of the gable wall) walls and around the top of the adobe walls. On the east and west side some of this stainless steel is 66 feet Long! The stainless steel will be locked into the all-thread steel rods which were drilled earlier into the wall of the adobe building. This will serve to tie the entire roof system together and prepare the roof for the eventual placement of roof sheathing and then shingles. Construction on the roof continued this week and last. The idea that a new roof would soon be on this building in the near future was amazing! Everyone was so happy with the pace of the project and once the new roof is on… completion of Phase 1 will be nearly complete.

    This week, September 2-5, the DCU crew completed the installation of all the stainless steel and the ridge blocks. The ridge blocks sit in between the rafters. On the exterior, DCU crew member, Pancho Villa, back filled the voids created by the ridge blocks with adobe bricks. In the *cocina*, the all thread rods were inserted from the *cocina* wall. This will help stabilize the exterior wall.

    Yes, more work on the main roof continues through September 8-15, 2008. The plywood (27 sheets of plywood) was installed on the entire main building roof. At this point, due to inclement weather the plywood was covered by tarps. Next up is the installation of the roof under-layment upon which the cedar shingles will be paced in the coming weeks. The fascia boards and overhangs have also been installed on the building. September 22-26 continued with more roof work. On the main part of the roof, the plywood had been placed and nailed off. The next step installed the 30 lb. felt, which will make the roof water tight. By now, all the cedar shingles had been delivered and awaiting installation. First, on the east elevation overhang, the new roof shingles were installed on the 1 inch by 4 inch redwood sheeting strips that had been placed on the 4 foot by 8 foot sheets of plywood and shingling continued on the main roof.

    In early October the DUC crew began the task of raising the balcony roof on the east side of the building. In one of the many restoration/rehabilitations in the 1950s, the front balcony was reconstructed incorrectly and resulted in a balcony with limited headroom and a dangerously low balustrade. Raising the roof involved tearing off the old rafters and sheeting and raising the roof 13 incnes. New 4 foot by 4 foot redwood beams were installed along with new 2 by 4 redwood rafters. The balustrade remained for now but will eventually be replaced in a later phase of the project. Other ongoing work during this time included work on the east elevation overhang roof and completion of the construction and lime wash of the upper south wall.

By late October, 2008, the roof on the balcony was completed. The balcony had been raised 13 inches, close to its original height and can now accommodate a standing person. The next phase of the project included restoring the balustrade and posts of the balcony, but for now it will remain with blocks in place to support the new roof slope. Other work that followed during this time on the Castro Adobe included finishing the roof shingle installation on the rear overhand and the balcony roof and finishing shingling the main part of the roof.

The massive restoration of the Castro Adobe has essentially been completed and everyone concerned with the project was completely happy with the beautiful new, safe building which evolved. Surely it will be an enlightening experience to view and visit the reconstructed building. At this juncture, one can only hope that the proposed State Park closings proposed by the Governor of California will circumvent the beloved Castro Adobe.

The Hansen house has also recently undergone an extensive renovation. Although almost completely modernized, it still contains the old metal roof. It is owned by Virginia McClune who lives there between visits to her daughter in Southern California. It along with the Castro Adobe has quite a history, although not as many inhabitants. Her son Randy operates the old neon shop just behind the Hansen house.

The Hansen house's name was derived from Hans Hansen, who built the house soon after the 1909 earthquake, when the Castro Adobe was damaged, and the Hansen family feared to live there any longer. During the the Loma Prieta earthquake, the Castro Adobe was seriously damaged but the Hansen house was not. The owner was very happy how the house held up during this event, especially when other houses and structures around the area were damaged.

TEN

It has been quite gratifying to follow the contemporary chronology of the Castro Adobe as has been presented in some of the chapters above, but it is also interesting to go back into early history, investigating some of the stories written concerning the Castro Adobe. One of interest is an account by Eliza Wood Farnham, written in 1850, probably in August, as she traveled from San Francisco back to her home in Santa Cruz. Eliza took a route down through the present Santa Clara valley, almost to the San Juan Bautista Mission, but before reaching it she turned southwest. Henry A. Hyde, writing in the 1930s, says that the first road through the Pajaro Valley was from the San Juan Mission to the Santa Cruz Mission. From that we can infer that this journey was one frequently taken by travelers between the two missions. Because Eliza was bringing a wagon from San Francisco to Santa Cruz, this would have been her best route. Following are excerpts from Chapter XII of *The Castro Rancho,* describing her visit of that time:

> Next night we reached Murphy's ranch, eighteen miles from San Juan, where we were kindly entertained. The following day we had only reached the beautiful valley of San Juan at three p.m. An American had told us that we could find comfortable quarters at Castro's rancho, about eighteen miles further on, and thither we went our way. It was nightfall before we reached neighborhood he had indicated...we descried a light which appeared to be twice that distance away and quite off the road. There was no choice but to steer for it, and stop at it too, whether it was the rancho or not. When we reached, which we succeeded in doing partly by following, in their zigzag course over the plain, we met the ghosts of three horsemen who were now bound thither, and we learned that Castro's rancho was still two miles away, but that we could stay there for the night. On the ground, under the corridor that ran along the old adobe building, two immense fires were blazing, around which were gathered twenty or thirty men and women, and several mules and horses.
>
> The kitchen was an apartment...eighteen by twenty-four feet, lighted only by a door in daytime, and, at this hour, by the fitful blaze of the wooden-fires, built upon a sort of brick range that ran across the end of the room...an Indian girl was making tortillas-the bread of the country...Beside her, upon two adobe jambs, which rose some fourteen or eighteen inches above the level of the range, lay a huge circular plate of iron--a rude griddle... At the other end of the range, a buxom, merry-faced

girl was superintending a pot of *caldo*, and another of *frijoles*... Five or six other young women were sitting or standing about, and several more were passing in and out to other parts of the *casa*...

I was called to supper in a long, spacious room or hall, at the upper end of which stood two beds. The long table occupied one entire side near the wall; but the cloth, to my surprise, was laid on only a small portion of it, with the plates for but half a dozen persons. The two proprietors were seated at it, and the younger man, also, but no female. When we were seated, the senior man threw each a tortilla from a stack that was piled on the cloth near his plate, and, helping himself, signed us to do likewise, the supper was delicious.

Of course there could be little conversation at supper, but I conveyed, in answer to their inquiries, very explicit information that Tom was not my husband; that I lived in Santa Cruz, and was on my way thither from San Francisco; and, in return, was informed that they were *hermanos* (brothers)...and that the young people were their nephews, nieces, and dependents of all sorts.

The supper was a far more palatable one than I believed it could be. The *caldo* was deliciously flavored; the tortillas very sweet and crisp; and everybody knows the frijole so well, that praise of it would be superfluous. When we had supped, I retired again to the kitchen, and here I found all the young people taking their evening meal, quite informally seated upon the earthen floor about the room. Two or three large basins, placed in various parts, contained the food, from which each supplied his or her palate at will... I directed Tom to have the horses ready and call me very early in the morning. "I will go home for breakfast," I said, "it is but sixteen miles."

The sleeping-apartment was in the second story, to which I mounted by a sort of ladder, constructed by tying bits of wood upon two poles with thongs of green hide, and placed against the sill of the door. The chamber was the entire size of the building, and was used as closet, store-room and granary. Two beds occupied the nearer end; wheat and barley the remote one, and sides of leather, old barrels, boxes, broken chairs, etc., the intermediate space. Zarapas of all styles were pendant from the roof, rafters, and walls. I objected to the door as lacking all means of fastening, but my solitude was promptly removed by the intelligence that six or eight persons were to share the apartment with me. The bed was not of the freshest, though everything upon it was snowy white. My sleep was unbroken til the words "The horses are ready, ma'am," sounded loudly in my ear next morning...and soon I descended equipped for departure...

    This then, was a Spanish rancho and the manner of life in it. These people were the owners of a great estate here, and another up the coast, on which were hundreds, if not thousands, of horned cattle and horses. Not a drop of milk nor an ounce of butter could be had in their house. Their chief articles of food are beef and beans.

    Of the wheat grown on their lands, they make a kind of coarse flour which they use in porridge. The tortilla can only be made of fine flour, which they have always imported... The simplicity of their external lives is quite in harmony with that of their natures. No ungratified want or cankering ambition, shorn of the power to achieve, consumes them...their whole manner...is so evident of kindness and respect, that there is nothing left to dread or doubt as to their motives. They are a simple-hearted people, whose contentment flowed out in acts of continual hospitality and kindness to all who came to them before their peaceful dream of life was broken in upon by the the frightful selfishness of the lated emigration. It is difficult for us to imagine contentment in the idle, aimless life of these rancheros, or cheerfulness in the dark, dirty, naked houses they inhabit; but they have sufficed for them, and it must be confessed that their domestic condition does not, in most parts of the country, promise any very rapid improvement from the example of their new neighbors.

From the previous excerpts, much can be learned about life at the Castro Adobe in the early 1850s. It was interesting to learn that the sleeping quarters were in the remote upper second-story, described as being reached only by a sort of ladder, constructed by tying bits of wood upon two poles with thongs of green hide. Because of the elaborate construction of the adobe, its three foot wide adobe brick walls and other heavy construction, it is certainly curious why a minor thing such as a stairway had not been previously constructed, such as the outside stair and inside staircase as were done in later years. What an effort it must have been to have had to climb that frail ladder each night prior to bedtime.

    It is also interesting to also learn that within the sleeping quarters of the second-story floor space that it was intermingled with sides of leather, boxes, old barrels, broken chairs, etc., and that wheat and barley was stored in the open space there as well. One might wonder at this point how the heavy wheat and barley and other things were transported up to the second floor; surely not via the frail ladder.

Perhaps during this era they had incorporated a pulley and rope system for this endeavor, but this we do not really know.

If future owners and inhabitants of the Castro Adobe could have looked back in time and have seen the activity in the kitchen as it was then in 1850, they would no doubt have been totally amazed! Who could have imagined that what to them served as a quite garage during their time, could possibly at one time served as a lively kitchen back then, an apartment-like quarters, eighteen by twenty-four feet, lighted by an open door at day time and at night by the fitful blaze of the wooden fires built upon a sort of brick range that ran across the total end of the room.

Then too, at the other end of the range, upon two adobe jambs, which rose some fourteen or eighteen inches above the adobe range, they could have seen a huge circular plate of iron, serving as a crude griddle. And additionally, across the end of the room could have been seen an Indian girl making tortillas and at the other end two other girls busy cooking, and at the same time five or six young women standing or moving about, and several more passing in and out to other parts of the *casa*. It would have been seldom that one failed to observe about these large haciendas some four or five musicians, who delightfully played. All this would have been hard to imagine

On April 10, 1920, an article entitled *Ned's Getaway* appeared in the *Santa Cruz Surf* which sheds more light on the history of the Castro Adobe. It is excerpted from *Narrative of Edward McGowan* and is an interesting pen picture of a Santa Cruz Hacienda (Castro Adobe) in the days of the fifties. It describes Ned McGowan's escape from the San Francisco Committee of Vigilance of 1856. McGowan was thought to have been an accomplice of James Casey, who in May 1856 killed James King, editor of the San Francisco *Evening Bulletin*. Casey was hung by the Vigilantes, while McGowan went into hiding, and was eventually acquitted in June 1857. McGowan stayed at the Castro Ranch on Sunday night June 29, 1856, leaving the following afternoon. The excerpt from the *Narrative of Edward McGowan* follows, with Edward McGowan (Ned) and his friends Dennison and Ramon in route to Santa Cruz from San Francisco:

> We were to travel...as far as the city of Santa Cruz, distant forty miles from the Pescadero. On arriving within about a half mile of the town, Dennison proposed that I should wait outside while he and Ramon went in to reconnoiter. It was desirable if possible to pass Santa Cruz without going through it...

On the outskirts on the other side we fell in with one of the brothers Castro (Rafael), a family well known in that section of the State. He was a relative of Ramon Valencia and appeared delighted to see him. Dennison told him the old story about my being an American priest, unable to speak Spanish, which was of course enough to ensure me his good will and respect.

This Castro sympathized with the Vigilance committee. His reason for it was that he thought it was a demonstration against the judges and lawyers. He had been subjected to many vexatious law suits, as he said, and besides disliked los Yankes, as he called Americans. We soon parted company with this gentleman and rode on until we reached the hacienda (San Andrés Rancho) of his brother, distant some fifteen miles from the city of Santa Cruz where we stopped for the night. This hacienda was, in itself, quite a little village. The mansion, although built of adobe, was unlike the generality of California houses. It has been built since the acquisition of the country by the Americans, a large, well-finished two story house. What particularly struck me about it was the ceiling of the upper rooms, which was composed of the most beautiful colored wood. There were, in all, some fifty persons about the premises.

These were the daughters, sons-in-law, and other relatives of the master (Juan Jose Castro), together with his dependents, servants, etc. As soon as we entered the house our host embraced his relative Ramon, welcomed us very kindly. Our horses were cared for, and after we had partaken of a fine repast the old gentleman invited us upstairs into a sort of a drawing room or parlor.

Here we found a large number of persons of both sexes, who seemed to be gathered there at an evening party. Our host directed some upon instruments for the amusement of the household. It being Sunday night, after 9 o'clock the dancing commenced. Thus the evening passed off very pleasantly.

While at breakfast the next morning the old gentleman, Dennison, who interpreted, asked me a great many questions. He asked me, among other things, how old I was. I told him forty-three. He replied that I must be at least sixty. "Why," said he, "I look younger than you, and I am fifty-five." I should suppose from his appearance that that was about his age. He was very large, probably weighing from 200 to 225 pounds. I must have looked much older than forty-three, for my beard was quite white, and I had not shaved for six weeks. As there was no necessity, however, for deceiving him with regard to my age, I told him the truth--that I was forty three. He said that he had observed that Americans to be like women in that respect--that they never told their real age.

We remained at the hospitable mansion of the old gentleman nearly all that day, waiting for one of his sons to get ready, who was to accompany us as far as San Luis Obispo, a distance of 200 miles. He was going in search of a younger brother and they were anxious to get him back. Mr. Castro's family is as fine a specimen of the old Californians as one would wish to see. The old gentleman himself, hale, hearty and robust, with a frank, manly countenance bespeaking the kindness and benevolence of his heart; his sons tall, active and graceful, and withal very intelligent. His wife, a good nature, amiable and lively old lady, still retaining the traces of her youthful beauty, while his daughters are possessed of all the bewitching little graces of mind and body which make the Spanish beauty so irresistible.

Long shall I remember the happy hours of respite from sorrow and anxiety which I enjoyed under that hospitable roof, and I here again and again thank them from the bottom of my heart for their kindness to me.

At length, young Castro being ready and having caught four fine horses for his journey, we bade adieu to our kind host and hostess, and in the cool of the afternoon again departed on our way.

Ned McGowan's journey from San Francisco to the Castro Adobe took place in mid-1856, around six years after a similar trip taken by Eliza W. Farnham, also previously related above. It is interesting to compare the descriptions of the second-story configuration of the Castro Adobe at these two different times, described by the two different travelers.

Eliza described mounting the second-story of the Castro Adobe by a sort of ladder, constructed by tying bits of wood upon two posts with thongs of green hide, and placed against the sill of the door. Here she found an open chamber the size of the entire lower building, being used as a storeroom for granary with two beds at one end. Also in the room were boxes, barrels, sides of leather and broken chairs, etc. in the immediate space.

On the other hand, Ned's story six years later tells of a large number of persons of both sexes he saw then and that dancing commenced after nine o'clock. In later writings, dancing was mentioned as being held on the upper-story called the fandango room, and makes us believe the dancing was probably done upstairs at this time too. It is unimaginable that the many guests gathered here in party cloths and climbed the ladder that Eliza described; surely a staircase must have been installed by then, and perhaps the upper room cleared for dancing. On the other had, it may have been a crude staircase, because later it is known that Hans said he built an upper story access for the family's convenience. At this time, Margaretta is seen holding Hanna on the veranda with no outside staircase to the veranda; no doubt there was an inside staircase that later was removed, because an outside staircase appeared later.

ELEVEN

Many have been concerned about the fate of the Castro Adobe in the past years, especially when it is now the last of five adobes that once doted this area. And fortunately, as we see above the last of the adobes in this area, the Castro Adobe, has been saved. Many people were responsible and involved in the restoration of this great structure; all should be greatly thanked. Following is an article, *Pajaro Valley's Last Adobe*, written in 1908 by Howard K. Dickson and which describes the early surrounding of the present Castro Adobe and its condition years ago:

> On one of the rolling hills of San Andrés stands Pajaro Valley's last adobes. Its gray walls have been streaked by the rains of many winters, and yet they stand there, to defy the storms of many more. Here and there a crumbling brick has dropped out of place, or the whitewash plaster is parted by long cracks. All these signs point, both to the time it was built, and forward to the day it will fall in ruins.
>
> In the year 1844, while Pajaro Valley was a wild, unsettled country, Castro obtained a grant of what is now known as the San Andres, or Castro Rancho. Here he built his adobe, about four miles west of present city of Watsonville, and on the ridge of the hill which forms east side of the present Larken Valley. The site was only a short distance from an old stage road, which then ran between Santa Cruz and southern points. Here Juan Castro lived in peace and ease. Hundreds of cattle grazed on his unfenced range, and the stage, with its guests and news, passed his very door.
>
> Time passed on. Pajaro Valley changed from a huge cattle range, owned by a few Spaniards, to a lively little valley of comparatively small ranches. Juan Castro passed away, and the San Andrés Rancho became the property of Mr. Rodriguez. He, in turn, after much of his land had been taken from him, sold the Castro Adobe and some surrounding land to the present owner, Mr. Hansen.
>
> Now, as we climb the hill and near the old building it still suggests something of its old-time grandeur. It stands there, one hundred feet long, fifty feet wide and thirty high, facing the present city of Watsonville. There are two wide porches, one for the first and the other for the second story, extending along almost the whole length of the building. These porches are very low and are supported by huge veranda posts. They help

to give the house a homelike appearance. Old rose bushes are climbing up over the porches and in front of them is an old-fashioned flower garden, surrounded by a garden fence. The flowers were planted within the past fifteen years, however. in the time of Juan Castro there was nothing about the mansion which would cut off his view from the surrounding land, save an old mission grapevine, twined itself around the veranda post and found its way to the roof. From the middle of each porch a small double door leads into the house. On each side of the doors, both upstairs and down, are two small windows. These windows still contain some of their original six-by-six inch glass. The house is bare at both ends, but at the back roof protrudes, forming another porch. Three doors open from the various rooms out upon this back porch.

Going into the house from the front door, we first find ourselves in a large room. This was originally part of a yet larger apartment. In the past few years the larger room has been divided off into a number of small ones. When Juan Castro used it, it was probably fifty feet long and twenty wide. It was his parlor and sitting-room combined. At the north of this room is a door leading into a somewhat smaller room, yet one which is of the width of the house. This room was probably Juan Castro's dining-room, as the kitchen adjoins it on the north.

The kitchen is a large room, built of rougher material than that of the house, and in the shape of a small addition to it, since the upper story does not extend over the kitchen. In this old kitchen one may yet see how Juan Castro cooked his food. The walls are even now black with the soot from the smoke of his open fire. Along one side of the room is a small bench of stone. Over this the wood was piled and the fire kindled. From chains swinging from the rafters above the kettles were hung. After the fire had gone out, bread was baked on the hot stones of the bench. A stairway now leads to the upper floor from the lower porch to the upper, on the outside of the house.

When we go up the stairs from the dining-room we first pass through a number of small rooms. But as we go toward the center of the house, we come into a large room which, before it was divided off, was fifty by twenty-five feet. This was the ball-room of the San Andrés Rancho. From the presence of the floor, it must have been used a great deal, for the surface is smooth and the boards, which are of good lumber, are nearly worn through.

How different now is the scene from the upper porch from that during Castro's day. Now we stand beside an old veranda post and look off over the old rancho. It is dotted with numerous farm-houses, surrounded by a few acres of plowed land or orchard, little pasture and less woods. Looking toward the east we see, directly in front of the house, only four miles away, the city of Watsonville. Behind the city we see the Gabilan and Santa Cruz mountains. To the north we look across numberless orchards, until our eyes finally reach Loma Prieta in the background, the sentinel of the pleasant valley.

All is new, the busy town, the sunny farms and the spreading orchards, all except the old, rolling mountains. However, they have come within the last fifty years to be somewhat even not the same. Their sides, almost bare, reflect the noonday sun, when once they were clothed with a forest of giant redwoods. But what did Juan Castro see when he and his friends looked from this same upper porch? To the west he saw his own San Andrés Rancho, with his own cattle grazing on it. The city of Watsonville was not in the east. In its place grazed the herds of other Spanish cattle kings, who lived in other adobes in the valley. Loma Prieta and Fremont's Peak looked down, as they do today, but now they see one adobe; then five. Where are the others now? Three fell in ruins because of lack of care, and now but a mound of earth shows where they once stood. Only a year ago one was torn to pieces because the owner thought that it concealed gold, and now but one is left. The present owner, through his interest in the early history of his state, vows that this last remnant of early California life shall not go to ruin while he lives and can preserve it. A new roof has been put on. Iron cobbles have been fastened from side to side, so as to hold the walls together. In fact, the building is so well braced that the earthquake of 1906 did not harm it. If it continues to be cared for, it will doubtless stand for many years. Yet one man's life is short. What will become of the old mansion when its present protector is gone? May it not then fall, as the others have, because of the lack of interest on the part of the people in early California history?

However, since the above words were written, "perhaps falling as have other adobes have"--is now looked upon as having to be perhaps remaining with us, instead of falling. By observation of the following Chain of Title prepared by Robert Becher, former Curator of Manuscripts, Bancroft Library, we see that the Castro Adobe has remained with us throughout a century plus:

1823 Arguello to Jose Joaquin Castro (provisional concession).

1833 Grant from Figueroa to Jose Joaquin Castro.

1846 Macedonia Lorenzana (2nd alcalde, Villa de Branciforte) to the heirs of Jose Joaquin Castro (judicial possession and official measurement of the grant).

1856 U.S. confirmation of Rancho San Andrés to Guadalupe Castro.

1872 Judgement v. Guadalupe Castro et al. in Castro v. Amesti awarding one third of Rancho San Andres to Amesti, plus costs and damages.

1873 Partition of Rancho San Andrés per map of T.W. Wright giving Juan Jose Castro 39 acres (Lot 3) containing Castro Adobe.

1874 Execution of judgement Vs. Juan Jose Castro for $36.35 upon sheriff's sale of the Castro Adobe and 39 acres (Lot 3, Wright survey of the County of Santa Cruz 1873) for $2,000. Sheriff Orton to William Patterson of San Francisco.

1879 Patterson to Albert B. Patrick of San Francisco,

1897 Declaration of Homestead by Hans Hansen.

1914 Hansen to C.I. Schueller.

1915 Schueller to Ada Westphal and husband.

1917 Westphal to Meda L. Waite and husband.

1924 Waite to Manuel E. Madiros (Manderos) and wife.

1929 Mandiros (Manderos) et al. to First National Bank of San Jose (deed of trust).

1935 First National Bank of San Jose to Frank Mello and Ann Elizabeth Mello.

1936 Declaration of Homestead by Frank and Ann Elizabeth Mello.

1937 Ann Elizabeth Mello to Frank Mello.

1938 Frank and Mary Mello right-of-way for gas and electricity.

1940 Frank Mello to Frank Mello, Jr., and wife.

1940 Vivian Mello to Frank Mello Jr.

1943 Frank Mello, Jr., to Alvin R. Holtzclaw and wife.

1945 Alvin R. Holtzclaw to George W. Holtzclaw and wife.

1948 George W. Holtzclaw to William M. Nelson and S. Maude Nelson.

1959 S. Maude Nelson to John K. & Suzanne Paizis.

1963 John K. Paizis to Victor A. & Sidney Jowers.

1968 Sidney E. Jowers to Elizabeth Lyman Potter.

1988 Elizabeth Lyman Potter to Joseph R. and Edna E. Kimbro.

TWELVE

Although the above text gives a chronological rendition of the inhabitants and events of the Rancho San Andrés Castro Adobe, it does not exploit much concrete evidence about the lives and activites of the early Castro families. But fortunately a recent Historic Structure Report was completed in 2003 by the following: Edna E. Kimbro, historian; Elizabeth Moore, architect; and Karen Hildebrand; archaeologist for California State Parks, Monterey, which brings to view pertinent historical information about these pioneer Castro families. Exerpts from this report presented below are very beneficial in establishing data which had not previously been firmly available .

The Rancho San Andrés Castro Adobe is a new aquistion of California State Parks and the only State Historic Park in the 72% Hispanic Pajaro Valley. There are no other historical landmarks or interpretive facilities that reflect the ethnic background of the majority of the community so well for family history. The acquistion of Rancho San Andrés Castro Adobe was consciously made to preserve and interpret the only remaining building of the Mexican Rancho era of California remaining in the Pajaro Valley, the finest example of a rancho hacienda in the Montery Bay region. The goal of this park unit will be to increase awareness of the Mexican Rancho era and interpret it for all the residents of the valley, a culturally diverse community in the State of California.

The Rancho San Andrés Castro Adobe is State Historic Land Marker number 998 and listed in the National Register of Historic Places. Therefore, it becomes historically significant for its association with the pioneer settlement of its families to be exploited and their histories to be brought forth in more detail than which has so far been presented.

The period of significace identified for the Rancho San Andrés Castro Adobe was with their Native American employers who built and inhabited the Castro Adobe. The outstanding character-defining features that distinguished this building included the spacious fandango room on the second floor, the *cocina*, one of five such original Mexican kitchens remaining in the state, and the Monterey Colonial arhitectural style of the Mexican era in California as typified by the two stories and the balcony.

The Castro family led by patriarch Joaquin Isidro Castro was among the founding settlers of Alta California who marched with Anza in 1775-1776 along the historic Anza Trail from Mexico. Expedition Padre referred to him as a soldier recriuit from Tubac in Sonora. Castro members with their ages of the Anza Expedition were: Joaquin Isidro de Castro, 48; Maria francisco, 50; Francisco

Antonio, 9; Jose jaoquin, 7; Carlos Antonio, 6 months; Ana Josefa, 18; and Maria Martina, 6.

In 1776 Joaquin Isidro Castro and familuy went to the Presidio of San Francisco, then Castro and his wife with their younger children were still settlers at Pueblo de San Jose as shown by the census of that year. Several of their sons were resident at the Presidio of Monterey in 1790, including Jose Joaquin Castro. A change occured in 1795 when the families of Joaquin Isidro Castro and his son-in-law Jose Maria Soberanes were granted provision concession by Governor Arguello of the Rancho Buena Vista near present-day Spreckles in the Salinas Valley. After Joaquin Isidro Castro died in 1801, his second oldest son Marino and his widow Martina went to Monterey where their oldest daughter lived. He was interred January 1, 1802.

Joaquin Isidro Castro's son, Jose Joaquin Castro and family were among the veterans who came to settle the new community of Villa de Branciforte in 1798. Jose Joaquin had served his country for 13 years as a soldier and was retiring. He came with his wife Maria Antonia Amador and two children. Records ahow that he sowed grain at Branciforte as early as 1799. Jose Joaquin Castro and his wife, Maria Antonia Amador, had a residence at the Villa de Branciforte, precise whereabouts unknown. According to a letter from Father Ramon Olbes in 1821 it was located in an out-of-the-way place in Branciforte, not on the main street. In 1827 and 1829 the family was still resident on that property.

Jose Joaquin Castro worked both at Branciforte and the Pajaro Valley. Record shows that he was paid $15 by Father Marcelino Marquinez of Mission Santa Cruz for unknow services rendered. In the early 1800s planting was done on the Pajaro Valley by the Brancifortians and the supplies charged at Mission Santa Cruz. Indians were rented at $4 per month each for sowing purposes. Accounts indicated that Jose Castro rented mission neophytes to sow fields in 1807. It appeared that these were Castro's fields at this time.

In 1804, census of Monterey included Jose, his wife and child who usually resided at the Villa de Branciforte. In 1808 census listed all of the belongings of the settlers, which gives insight into the material wealth of Jose Joaquin Castro and his family and indicates that he still lived in the Villa de Branciforte. The Santa Cruz History Journal has shown his censes at this time owing 150 cows, 25 mares, 30 horses and 20 mules. Castro and Maria Amador had a child named Jose Ignacio who died that year and was buried at Mission San Juan Bautista. Apparently his parents were with Mariano at Los Animas (Rancho de la Poza). The following year, 1812, Carlos Castro, younger brother of Jose Joaquin Castro, was mayor domo of Mission Santa Cruz.

Jose Joaquin followed in his brother's footsteps and in 1818 was mayor domo, or employee, at Mission Santa Cruz. On October 16, 1818 Father Olbes wrote to Governor Sola saying that the mayor domo (Jose Joaquin Castro) is actually residing at the mission. At the time of the Bouchard raid of Monterey, the Brancifortians raided Mission Santa Cruz causing Castro and Commisionado Joaquin Buelna no end of consternation. Olbes went to Mission Santa Clara and refused to return because he was so enraged at the behavior of the low-life Brancifortians who sacked the mission establishment themselves, thinking that their depredations would be blamed upon the Argentinian privateer who failed to appear. This was an instance in which the bad reputation of the Brancifortians was found warranted.

In 1821 Father Olbes wrote to Governor Pablo Vicente Sola complaining that Joaquin Castro (Jose Joaquin Castro after his father's death was often referred to just as Joaquin) was being unfair to Francisco Gonzales (Corporal of the Escolta) and Serafin Pinto (his brother-in-law) in trying to prevent them from building houses in Branciforte on sites selected by Olbes. Olbes goes on to report that the Brancifortians have not built their houses in orderly rows around a square (as called for by the plan of Pitic). He says that Joaquin Castro's house is among the most distant and poorly situated. He went on to report on the locations of others that are entirely hidden for gambling, etc. He suspects that Castro is trying to obstruct Gonzales from becoming a settler of Branciforte because he does not want another respected man in the community. This confirms that Joaquin Castro had a home in Branciforte and that it was not on North Branciforte Avenue at the head of Water or Soquel Avenues where the priests desired.

Following the Mexican War of Independence from Spain, Governor Arguello granted conditional possession to Jose Castro of Rancho San Andrés, to Jose Amesti of Rancho Corralitos, and to Francisco Haro of Rancho Salsipuedes, making the beginning of the rancho era in the Pajaro Valley. The application for the grant of Rancho San Andrés was in the names of Joaquin Castro and his son-in-law Francisco de Sales Rodrigues married to Rafaela Castro. In 1827 Joaquin and his family still resided in the Villa de Branciforte, despite their rancho as indicated by the census. Juan Jose Castro, Joaquin Castro's son had a large family, but did not petition for his own land grant.

Also in 1828 a census of heads of households and their belongings was compiled. Joaquin Castro and son were listed consecutively and the same amount of assets were listed for them; therefore, it is supposed that they shared their assets. A total of 32 heads of families were listed. Joaquin Castro's and son's were: 14 oxen; 1 house; 500 cows; 20 horses; 6 mules; 2 carrelas; and 4 mares.

On January 1, 1831, Jose Joaquin Castro was alcalde (chief political officer) of Branciforte. Election of alcalde was an honor and responsibilty conferred upon honorable men of the community. Five years later the 1836 census indicated changes in residence, perhaps as a result of Governor Jose Figueroa having re-granted or confirmed Rancho San Andrés to Joaquin Castro in 1833 at secularization. At this time no Castros were listed in town; many of the ranchos in Santa Cruz County had already been granted as a result of secularization of Mission Santa Cruz.

Tradition says that Maria Rosario Briones was 14 when she and Castro married in 1830. She was born January 18, 1816. In different accounts, historian Rowland gave three different years for her marriage: 1830, 1832, and 1833. The last two children of hers listed in a previous census were hers by Joaquin Castro. Following this 1936 census she had another son by Joaquin named Jose Ricardo del Refugio Castro born April 3, 1836, and baptized on April 4 of the same year at Mission Santa Cruz. She had yet another child by Joaquin Castro at Mission Santa Cruz in January of 1838, Jose de los Reyes, who died in that same year as did his dad, Joaquin Castro. She married Jose Julian Espinosa November 24, 1838 at Mission San Juan Bautista two months after her husband's death. Rosario's mother was Maria Antonia Vasquez making her Maria Rosario Briones y Vasquez before her marriage. She was one quarter Indian.

By 1836 the other children of Jose Joaquin were residing on their own ranchos or those of their spouses. The daughters married young. Maria de Los Angeles was aged 16 and lived at Rancho San Augustin with sister Candida Bolcoff. Jacinta lived with the Bolcoff family too before joining the convent at Monterey.

Jose Joaquin dated his will at the rancho 25 days before his death in 1838 when he died of smallpox. He was buried next to his first wife beneath the floor of the Santa Cruz Mission church in a Franciscan habitat. It would be possible that Joaquin had the Rancho San Andrés Castro Adobe built for his bride before 1836 as many have claimed, but for irrefutable physical evidence to the contrary.

The first two-story residential (non-mission) adobes date to 1834-35 in Monterey (Alvarado and Larkin). Given relationships and the fact that Larkin was alredy contracting for lumber and shingles at this time, this one could have come along right aferwards.

However, the extant records of 1830 and 1846 do not depict the Rancho San Andrés Castro Adobe. They show only the earlier adobes and the corral over near the bay on San Andreas Road. This is one of the main reasons why the adobe is thought to have been built later by son Juan Jose Castro.

Clearly Joaquin Castro no longer owned a home in Branciforte or in the vicinity of Mission Santa Cruz in 1838 or he would have bequeathed it in his will. He proabably previously sold it or gave it to one of his children before 1838. There is no record of any such transaction extant.

In his will Joaquin Castro left his second wife one hundred head of cattle, one room of his current house and cooking untinsels, if she did not remarry. If she did, which she did to Julian Espinosa, she gave up her share to their son Ricardo which was to be administered by Guadalupe and Juan Jose, son of Jose Joaquin. Rosaria did not take this lyning down. She filed a suit for a part with John Gilroy as advocate in 1839 and ended up receiving child support payments until 1844. She requested an inventory of the personal property left by Joaquin Castro to her on February 28, 1839. Januaary 27, 1840 she had Juan Jose and Guadalupe Castro summoned to San Juan Bautista to appear in court. In 1852 she contested the will, an action which ended with the 1856 partition of Rancho San Andrés into shares, none of which she received.

Joaquin Castro left his son Ignacio 100 head of livestock as he did his dughter Jacinta who became a nun in 1851. The livestock and a lot she owned in Santa Cruz granted to her in 1840 constituted her dowry after she entered St. Catherin's Convent as sister Rosa. She provided the Dominican nuns the $2,000 it provided from the sale of her property with which they purchased their convent building in Monterey together with the bishop.

Ignacio was also given use of the *carreta* and oxen until such time as he had his own. Joaquin indicated that the other emancipated children had already gotten their share of livestock. He directed that the balance of the livestock be divided between married daughters Maria Antonia, Martina and Candida. To son Guadalupe, his first executor, he left the mill and the stud Jackass for the bendfit of all. Son Juan Jose was named second executor.

The 1839 census shows that there were still three separate households. Only one rancho was listed, that of Amesti. Indians were listed separately and last. The Castro family was probably all living on the rancho because of their occupations and the fact that they owned it for some years already. Maria Rosario Briones de Castro must have remarried already because she and her children were gone. On May, 1840, Juan Jose Castro registered brand and ear marks with David Spence, Alcalde of Monterey--a sure sign that he had cattle.

There were four separate Castro households on Rancho San Andrés in 1843. We know from reports that there were two houses over by Monterey Bay, Guadalupe's planting shack near Freedom Blvd. in 1839, and supposedly Joaquin's place near the Pajaro River of the 1812 era. The existence and nature of the 1812 era place is not well established. It may have been made up by the sons later to support the contention of a Sola era concession.

However, if Guadalupe were in the planting shack, and Ygnacio and Joaquin over by the bay, Juan Joase and his large number of children and servants could have been resident in the Rancho San Andrés Castro Adobe, but not conclusive. In 1841 it appears that brothers Guadalupe and Joaquin and Indian Ybon were all at the planting shack. Then Joaquin got married and was no longer with them in 1843.

There was plenty of Indian labor available on the rancho for a building project at this time in 1843 and 1844. 1844 is the estimated date of construction given by the grandchildren of the Castros (proably children of Manuel). They are the source of information about trouble with Indians at the other site by the bay and said that the Rancho San Andrés Adobe cost $30,000 to build. A survey form of April 1934 gives the approximate date of construction as 1844. Furthermore, Dirkson's article written about the adobe in 1908 when the Hansens owned it said that it was built in 1844. A possible date of construction of the Castro Adobe of 1843-44 has good support, but is not conclusive.

The adobe does not appear on 1846 reports. So, lacking any real conclusive evidence, a mid to late 1840s date for construction is postuated and judgement is reserved upon whether or not it was built in the 1830s for Joaquin's bride Rosaria or in 1844 by the Indian servants and employees. More evidence is needed to be certain. The 1845 census shows only two households on the rancho. Reported physical evidence presented elsewhere indicates that the adobe was built after 1847, proably in 1848-49 because embedded lumber is all circular sawn.

In the 1970s Robert Becker, Manuscripts Curator at the Bancroft Library wrote a piece about the Castro Adobe in which he speculated that it was built by Juan Jose Castro in the Gold Rush years of 1848-49. This would go along with local tradition about it costing $30,000, and having been built with money from the mines. Agusta Fink went along with this theory in *Adobes in the Sun*. The gold rush story seemed too be without any concrete evidence to support it. Since physical evidence is now in hand, Becker's date of 1848-49 is supported and accepted as the official date of construction. It is interresting to note that in the 1850 U. S. census Juan Jose listed a large net worth of $12,000. Perhaps this could reflect a trip to the mines.

In the spring of 1846, the boundaries of Rancho San Andrés were set by Second Alcalde Macedonio Lorenzana, an Indian from Mexico. There was a protest by Amesti after the fact, and an arbitration before Walter Colton was conducted with arbiters Juan B. Alvarado (president), Jose Abrego, Jose Rafael

Gonzales, William Hartnell, Milton Little, Juan Malarin and David Spence, in Monterey in 1847. The all Monterey businessman arbiters found results in favor of Amesti, except for Alvarado who expressed reservations about the injustice of the proceeding. The arbitration was conducted suspiciously like a trial which it was not supposed to be under Mexican law.

In 1850, the Executors of the estate of Jose Joaquin Castro sued Jose Amesti for possession of the contested land between them, and in 1851 the Superior Court of Santa Cruz County ruled in their favor. However, Amnesti then petitioned to overturn, but that was overruled by the court. Then Amnesti asked for a dismissal of the matter on grounds that the court of Walter Cotton had already considered the matter and that it was appealed to the Supreme Court of California, holding the land in jeopardy, making the land unusable for the Castros.

The complaint, filed by attorney Pacificus Ord, called the lanuage of Castro's 1846 proceeding descriptive of a jury trial and said, "Complainants took all the steps that diligence required to arrest this extraordinary proceeding but was unsuccessful, being poor, and having little or no influence against the powerful party of the said Jose de Amesti arrayed against them." A look back at the jury shows that it was a panel of proninent citzens and fellow merchants and neighbors of Jose Amesti. The property the
Castros hoped to recover and losst was tragic for them.

Juan Jose Castro and Guadalupe Castro were elected Justices of the Peace of the county in 1851. At the same time the Court of sessions acting as asessor reduced the value of San Andrés Rancho to $15,000 on August 25, 1851. The following year Juan Jose Castro was elected a Supervisor of Santa Cruz County, the first Hispanic one and the last until 2000.

In 1857 the U. S. Land Commission confirmed Rancho San Andrés to the heirs, but the 1860 survey reduced it to 8,911.53 acres. The Castros appealed the reduction in the rancho size in court but in 1867 Judge Hoffman confirmed the reduction. In April 7, 1864 the *Pajaronian* contained this information: Rancho San Andrés was one half under cultivation. There was a suit of partition in the U. S. District Court, <u>Briody vs. Hale</u>, involving F. Larkin, C. Miller, V. Westcott, A. Cox, C. K. Erambarck, A. Hughes and a large number of Castros. In an interview with Juan Jose Castro, he said that he had about 150 acres left, and had expended about $40,000 expenses in law suits.

In 1873 the Partition of Rancho San Andrés was completed by T. W. Wright. Manuel Castro was apporrtioned lot 9 of 41 acres on Larkin Valley Road. His uncle Guadalupe received lot 2 of 61.5 acres. Juan Jose got lot 3, 39 acres with the adobe. Ignacio's share (Ignacio was son of Ignacio who died in 1859) was lot 7, 50.5 acres. Siomon was a son of Ignacio and a grandchild of Jose Joaquin Castro who received lot 4, 34 acres. Joaquin Castro received lots 43 and 59. There were probably two Joaquin Castros at this time, one a son and another a grandchild.

On December 13, 1873 the Rancho San Andrés Adobe was sold to the highest bidder in front of the Courthouse, Lot #3, with 39 acres, for $2,000. This was Jaun Jose's lot and the Castro family hacienda. This execution was to recover court costs and damages in the trial of <u>Amesti vs. Executors of the Estate of Joaquin Castro.</u> Juan Jose's share of costs and damages was only $36.35. The attorney for the Amesti family, William Patterson of San Francisco, bought it for $2,000. Since the Castros owed $5,000 in damages in total, it is probable that the whole $2,000 went to help cover those costs. The other plaintiffs were also responsible for their share too. On June 24, 1874, Execution vs. Juan Jose Castro for $36.35 in gold coin was made referencing the 1873 sale. This represents the final date of legal loss of the Castro Adobe by Juan Jose Castro.

In 1875 Juan Jose Castro was listed as a farmer at Pajaro. There was indication that Juan Jose and his family stayed on as tenants of the new San Francisco owners. On January 30, 1877, Juan Jose Castro, aged 75, died and was buried in the Catholic Cemetery of St. Patrick's Church. The 1880 census reveals that Juan Jose's son stayed on as a tenant of the new owners of the Rancho San Andres Castro Adobe.

In 1893 Guadalupe, Juan Jose's brother, died at age 84. Juan Jose also had a son named Guadalupe. The *Santa Cruz Surf* of August 16, 1893, reported that Juan's brother Guadalupe was a manufacturer of guitars and violins as well as being a musician who played at parties or fiestas. Apparently there was an historical exhibit by the Native Daughters of the Golden West that featured the violin and guitar of Guadalupe Castro. Juan Jose was survived by his youngest brother Joaquin living at Gilroy and his step brother Ricardo living at Freedom.

Because Guadalupe was listed in the 1860 census as a carpenter and was a well known maker of musical instruments, it is supposed that he may have been the designer of his brother Juan Jose's home, the large two-story rancho hacienda, and that he may have fashioned the unusual wood floors..

According to historian Ed Martin: "Guadalupe Castro, who died a few years ago, one of the descendants of pioneer Joaquin Isidro Castro, used to amuse himself by writing to the authorities at Washington D. C. in support of his claim to the whole of Branciforte territory. He died in penury and want, his--Castles in the Air--never materialized." Another source said that he had actually gone to Washington D C. in the 1880s about his land titles.

Actually according to the reminiscences of Maria de Los Angeles Castro, 73, and Gaudalupe Castro, 81, states as mentioned in the Santa Cruz *Surf*, September 27, 1890, that Gaudalupe was philosophical about his loss of lands and called himself content. He was playing the guitar when the reporter arrived. He made violins and guitars in his work room in the old Majors mill where he resided across the street from his sister in Santa Cruz. He played a medley on the violin as well and spoke of playing for fandangos as far away as San Francisco. His sister, however, was embittered by her loss of land as were her 12 children.

Guadalupe received lot 2 next to Juan Jose and the family headquarters in the 1873 partition forced by <u>Briody vs. Hale</u>. On september 13, 1873, after the judgement in <u>Amesti vs. Castro</u>, lot 2 of 61 and one-half acres was sold in front of the courthouse for $750 to satisfy damages and court costs of the lawsuit. Guadalupe continued to live on the ranch with his young brother Ricardo until at least 1880 when he was 75, then went to live with his sister in Santa Cruz.

Close examination of land title records at the Recorder's office indicates that Guadalupe was something of an operator in his younger years. As Exequtor it appears that he was entitled to sell land on behalf of the estate which he did, often. In order to pursue their title to the rancho he sold their attorney W. W. Crane a portion of the rancho. He persuaded two of his sisters, Martina and Jacinta, to give up their portions of the rancho to him that he sold. Altogether it appears that he sold more of the rancho than finally existed making it absolutely necessary that the lawsuit against Amesti be won. Losing the lawsuit ensured the ruin of all. Jose Joaquin's son Ignacio died in 1859 and his widow remarried Matthew Fellom. His son Simon was apportioned 68 acres or lot 8 of Rancho San Andrés. His share was also up to help for the damages and court costs. Another Ignacio was apportioned lot 7 on the 1873 partition survey, probably his son Ignacio.

Juan Castro had two wives and many children by both; his younger brothers and their families often made their home with him. His home was the largest and finest adobe in the contry where his large family celebrated frequent fiestas dancing in his second floor fandango room. A number of sources say that bull and bear fights were held in a corral in front of the house and the hand wrought iron ring and tang exist to support the contention.

 Local tradition suggests that he built the Castro Adobe with money gotten during the gold rush. Several of his neighbors family members, Jose Bolcoff and Michael Lodge ,went to the mines as well; one source says that the valley was deserted in 1848. The possibility of a cash infusion from the mines may explain why he alone built a large residence.

Juan Jose was a tall, heavy man, nearly 300 pounds according to one source. He was elected to the highest public office in the county (Supervisor) in 1852 and appeaars to have merited respect, although no obituary was found for him. Larkin included him in his list of important men in the county, yet there is virtually no description of him in print that has been located. Unhappily, no photographs of him or any of his children have been found. Yet, the Rancho San Andrés Castro Adobe put his stamp and that of his family upon the land.

Juan Jose inherited one whole thirteenth part of the rancho in 1856. On June 21, 1855, Juan Jose sold all of his live stock to his wife for $2,000. Then, on August 14, 1855, he sold her all of his interest in the rancho for $3,000. Juan Jose again deeded his interest in Rancho San San Andrés to his wife January 1, 1870, for $3,000. The reasons behind these transfers are not clear, but may have to do with his second wife buying a community property interest in the rancho or Juan Jose trying to escape debt. Juan Jose sold Frank Larkin one half of one undivided thirteenth part of Rancho San Andrés on August 24, 1859, for $1,700. The following year on November 20, 1860, he sold Charles Ford one quarter interest. On the same day he recorded another similar deed. This must have been a duplicate recordation, otherwise it would have represented all of his remaining interest in one thirteenth of the rancho. October 25, 1861, Juan Jose sold 15.5 acres of Rancho San Andrés to Antonio Prider for $250.

In 1871 Santa Cruz County assessment records indicate that Juan Jose Castro was assessed for one undivided twelfth of San Andrés Ranch in Pajaro Township. He was in possession of 150 acres valued at $900. The house was valued at $200 and the furniture at $25 for a total of $1,125. The tax due was $33.46. Other transfers appear to be part of transactions necessary to pay lawyers to engage in law suits of Amesti, vs. Hale, and vs. Rosaria Briones Castro Espinosa. May 1, 1868, Juan Jose's wife sold all of her interest in 40 acres of the rancho for $200 to son Manuel.

Juan Jose seems to have been very hospitable in the circa 1850 Farnham narritive which appears to be about the Rancho San Andrés Castro Adobe. He sounds merry and affable in the Ned McGowan narrative of 1856 which is without doubt about the Rancho San Andrés Castro Adobe. He welcomed his brother Joaquin and his family into his home, sharing it in 1850. His oldest son Manuel married, stayed home on the rancho, and received land near by in the 1873 partition, lot 9. Juan Jose appears to have had a full life enjoying the fandangos, bull and bear fighting and active social life as the head of a very large extended family. We know that in 1864 before the partition in 1873 he had about 150 acres and had spent an estimated $40,000 on his lawsuit with Amesti and proving his title before the U. S. Land Commission. After the conclusion of the lawsuit and the division of the rancho, he had nothing and died poor in 1877, probably renting back the house and land from its absentee San Francisco owners as did his son Trinidad.

It has previously been reported in this writing that the Castro family came to settle in California in the Anza Expedition of 1775-6. Here we learned that Joaquin Isidro Castro and his wife Martina Boutillier and their children marched to California overland from Mexico through Arizona. However, census records reported that they were from Villa Sinaloa, but Font, chaplain for the expedition, said that they joined at Tubac in present day Arizona. The expedition stopped in Monterey at the Royal Presidio for some time, where Joaquin Isidro Castro's oldest daughter met and married Jose Maria Soberanes which started another major California family.

As early as 1801 Mariano Castro, the second oldest son of Joaquin Isidro Castro, proposed a colony that was to have six members: Jose Rodriguez; Juan Maria Ruiz; Delores Mesa; Joaquin Castro; Antonio Buelna; and Pablo Botero. Three of these heads of families were later founders of Branciforte in Santa Cruz. However, their eagerness to move to the Pajaro Valley reflects the lack of sowing lands in east Santa Cruz and the necessity of sowing along the Pajaro River that is reflected in the Libro de Cuentas of Missiion Santa Cruz in the early years.

The proposed colony served as the basis of Mariano's initial vice regal petition for Rancho La Brea in 1802. There was opposition to the vicroy's grant of La Brea from the missionaries of San Juan Bautista which explains Mariano and his aged mother still being in Monterey in 1804. On July, 1807, Jose M. Estudillo, Secretary to governor Arrillags, inquired of the Branciforte Comisionado if there would be a problem with colonists locating there.

The response is unknown but historians Milliken and Laffey indicate that Marioano succeeded in getting and occupying Las Animasin 1808-11, which explains the presence of Joaquin and Maria Amador at Las Animas in 1811. More interestig, it is consistent with the Castro's claims that their father had possession of Salsipuedes, Pajaro and Las Animas in 1812, ten leauges of of land. It is conceivable at this early date that Mariano and his brothers actually had the use of Salsipuedes on the Pajaro and Las Animas at one time; the lands are all contiguous, and not well differentiatd. The Castros claimed that their concession, occupied as early as 1812, was made by Pablo Vicente Sola in 1818. This is not as far fetched as it may seem because in Monterey, Sola made a number of gtants that were not recorded in any registers; we only know about them because they are referenced in later deeds.

Also it is important to recall that Joaquin Castro's name was prominent in the accounts of Mission Santa Cruz that name him often as sowing on the Pajaro in the early 1800s. Some justification for a right of claim may have formed from more than holey cloth or thin air. While the Castro family's claims were technically inaccurate because the lands referred to were well defined later in the rancho era and granted to others, early on the boundaries of provisional concessions, like that at Buena Vista, were not well defined.

Futhermore, in 1812 Estudillo wrote a report to Governor Arillaga about a controversy over pasture lands between the mission priests and the residents of the Villa de Branciforte. The mission priests claimed that the settler's pasture extended only to the Rio Soquel, whereas the settlers thought they extended to the Pajaro. The Brancifortians claimed that the mission had only temporary use of the pasturage at Aptos but had moved in on the area called San Antonio near Freedom and the San Andrés. They rounded up the mission's sheep from the San Andrés and took them to Aptos. They threatened the Indian sheperd Andres and burned his domicile. Estudillo wrote that Branciforte Comisionado Briones said that the mission sheep were pastured at Canada del Siervo located at Rancho San Andrés' eventual bountry with Rancho Corralitos. Estudillo sided with the Branciformians in this controversy. Finally in 1817 the Branciformians agreed to let Mission Santa Cruz use pasturage in the Pajaro Valley. It is possible that these events formed the basis of the Castro family's claims to using 10 leagues of land in the Pajaro Valley as early as 1812 and building a house there in that year. Historian Rowland seems to have thought so. This issue deserves further research.

Be that it may, in 1823 Governor Luis Arguello granted ranchos to three claimants in the immediate area: Jose Joaquin Castro for San Andres; Jose Amesti for Los Corralitos; and Francisco de Haro for the place called Salsipuedes. The latter rancho was mentioned in the Santa Cruz documents when the mission asked for the use of it from the Branciformians and they allowed the mission to put livestock there about 1817. Strickly speaking Salsipuedes was not considered a mission ranch, it had been the horse ranch of the Presidio of Monterey. After the Mexican revolution, it was up for grabs. The Castros did not grab enough, only as much as they did receive.

All this could be considered ancient history but it was the background or psychological baggage of Jose Joaquin Castro's sons, real or exaggerated. They knew that their grandfather, father and their uncles were considered founders of California and had controlled vast expanses of land. Rightly or wrongly, the point is this later generation of Castros felt cheated, actually beginning in the Mexican period when the land grant boundries were finalized. But they apparently traced their troubles back to Colton's Monterey court in 1846 and blamed the American judicial system. They appealed a finding for Amesti based on the jury members, everyone of whom was a peer of Amesti and lived in Monterey. They won and then Amesti appealed to the State Supreme Court. Reading judge Hoffman's 1867 decision confirming the survey that reduced Rancho San Andrés in size by about 4,000 acres, the argument about possession is consistently made in favor of Amesti despite the fact that he claimed twice as much land (4 leagues) as he was originally granted (2 leagues). Yet when the Castros clained more than 2 leagues, Hoffman judged that the land was all Amesti's despite the fact that the Castros had planted and lived on it and held the invocation of having possessed all the land thereabouts in times long past. Amesti claimed to have had the original house of Joaquin Castro (1812) and a dwelling of Guadalupe (1839) on the land in question which happened to be the only fertile land of the Castros grant, a key issue. In a Mexican court settlement of the land might have been divided between the two claimants as conciliation, being done to encourage promoting of goodwill and harmony.

The Castros pressed their claims through the American court system until potential remedies were exhausted and they were ruined by the court costs and fees of the Amesti attorneys and the damages awarded. They did so for the reasons above stated, righteous indignation combined undoubtly with a measure of greed. Little wonder Jose Joaquin's youngest son Joaquin took up with Tiburcio Vasquez, the social bandit supported by the Californios who robbed the Americans.

The following quote provided by Marion Pokriats is telling about the local American resentment of the land grantees:

> Gone are the days when the Castros, handsomely decked out in velvet and lace, would ride by on their silver palominos to be greeted as 'tin Gods' by the poverty stricken populace. A new era, one of intensive cultivation of the soil, was ushered in, it brought a romance of its own, less poetic perhaps, but built on a more substantial foundation than the preceding one.

We can assume that the poverty stricken populace referred to were the American squatters who made Prudencia Amesti's life a living hell as they stole and fenced off her land. Ed Martin's *History of Santa Cruz County* states that at the rancho Amesti a fort was erected, and that the squatters were determined to 'hold the fort' at all hazards. But that the strong arm of Uncle Sam was invoked and succeeded in restoring order and quieting titles.

The American majority had other ways of gloating. For example, news of the Hispanic pioneers of the area was not included in the early newspapers, except in the legal notices as they lost their land. Their births and deaths and social events were not reported. The 1864 story of Juan Jose Castro losing his land was reported verbatim three times, the last time in the 1879 county history, as though nothing else had happened on the rancho in fifteen years. Such indifference makes historical research of the first Hispanic settlement of the area difficult, and all the more necessary to do if the new majority is to understand its roots in Mexican California.

THIRTEEN

In her two newspaper interviews Maria de los Angeles Castro Majors was bitter. The Bolcoffs were probably bitter at the loss of Rancho Refugio and necessity of returning to San Andrés. Guadalupe appears to have been bitter for a time, but died content. Juan Jose was, but seems to have enjoyed a good life on the rancho and taken events in stride. Ignacio died young and missed the worst of it.

But Joaquin, the youngest son of Jose Joaquin Sr., who lived with his brother Juan Jose in the Castro Adobe in the 1850s had reasons to be bitter. Unlike Guadalupe, Juan Jose and Ignacio, he received no individual land grant or shared in Rancho San Andrés. His father died in 1838 when he was about 17. In 1839 and 1840 he was living with Guadalupe on Rancho San Andrés. He married about 1843 and lived in Branciforte, perhaps in his father's town home. In the 1850, 1860, and 1870 census he lived on the San Andrés. In 1847 he purchased a whip-saw from Thomas O. Larkin so he was presumably a sawyer, perhaps at Corralitos.

Larkin Valley near the Castro Adobe was named in honour of Thomas O. Larkin. Larkin was a resident of Monterey but he had holdings in real estate in other areas around the Monterey Bay area. He purchsed acreage from the Castros which included a portion of present day Larkin Valley.

Larkin was born in Charleston, Massachusetts, the son of Thomas O. Larkin and Ann Rogers, and a grandson of the Deacon John Larkin who provided the horse for Paul revere's famous ride. At age of 15, Larkin went to Boston to apprentice as a bookbinder but decided against the business. In 1821 he sailed to Wilimington, North Carolina, where he worked as a clerk and experienced a disastrous partnership with a dishonest merchant. He visited Bermuda in 1822 and relatives in New England in 1824. In 1825 he opened a store in Duplin, North Carolina. The fortune he maded on the strore he lost on a sawmill operation, and in 1830 he returned to Massachusetts, destitute. Here he learned that his half-brother, John Bautista Rogers Cooper, needed his assistance with a business in California, and in September 1831 Thomas left Boston on the ship *Newcastle*. After a stopover in the Sandwich Islands, he landed in San Francisco, in Aprill 1832.

Aboard ship, he met and developed an intimate relationship with Mrs. Rachel Hobson Holmes, who was coming to California to join her husband, Captain A. C. Holmes, a Danish seaman. They traveled together from San Francisco to Monterey where they both boarded at the Cooper house. When

Rachel learned she was carrying Thomas' child, she discreetly moved to Santa Barbara while Thomas remained in Monterey, working with his brother. At Santa Barbara Rachael gave birth and awaited a dreadful reunion with her husband, but within a few weeks, she learned her husband had died a year before while at sea en route to Lima, Peru.

Meanwhile, Larkin worked as a clerk for John B. R. Cooper until early 1833, when he was able to start a small store of his own and build a double-geared flourmill, the first of its kind on the West Coast. He was able to invest again in a sawmill, this time in Santa Cruz. He sailed to Santa Baarbara and there was reunited with Rachel. They were married there on board the American bark *Volunteer*. The U. S. Consul for the Sandwich Islands, John Coffin Jones, performed the ceremony and years later when it was didcovered he did not have the authority to perform the service, they had to be remarried.

In 1835 he built his wife a house in Monterey that mixed New England and California architectural styles. It became known as the Larkin House Adobe and is still extant today. It is believed by some historians that the Rancho San Andrés Adobe, constructed some several years later, was perhaps styled somewhat from the two-story Larkin House Adobe. Larkin built the first wharf for ships and was commissioned to rebuild the Monterey Customs House. He engaged in trade with Mexico, the Sandwich Islands and China.

Historian Theodore H. Hittell, in his *History of California*, noted that Thomas O. Larkin wrote from San Farancisco to James Buchanan, secretary of state at Washington, giving an account of a gold discovery. It was then several weeks since the gold had commenced to come in, and by that time about twenty thousand dollars worth had been exchanged for merchandise and provisions. He was the first and only American consul to the Mexican government and was a confidential agent of the U. S., trying to bring about American occupation of California without war.

This was the time of gold in California and when word reached Monterey of its existence many in the area went to the gold fields to claim their riches. It is certainly possible that the Castro family was enriched by some of this gold; and that perhaps it was used to finance the construction of the Rancho San Andrés Adobe, as some have proposed. At this point, it is perhaps well to relate an appropriate quote of Larkin's letter of June 1, 1848, to James Buchanan, showing what excitement was found in the gold fields and why the lure was so great. Larkin's letter follows:

Sir: I have to report to the State Department one of the most astonishing excitements and state afairs now existing in this country, that, perhaps has ever been brought to the notice of the Government. On the American fork of the Sacramento and Feather River, another branch of the same, and the adjoining lands, there has been within the present year discovered a placer, a vast tract of land containing gold, in small particles. This gold, thus far, has been taken on the bank of the river, from the surface to eighteen inches in depth, and is supposed deeper, and to extend over the country.

On account of the inconvenience of washing, the people have, up to this time, only gathered the metal on the banks, which is done simply with a shovel, filling a shallow dish, bowl, basket, or tin pan, and washing out the sand by movement of the vessel. It is now two or three weeks since the men employed in those washings have appeared in this town with gold, to exchange for merchandise and provisions. I presume nearly 20,000 dollars of this gold has as yet been so exchanged. Some 200 or 300 men have remained up the river, or are gone to their homes, for the purpose of returning to the Placer, and washing immediately with shovels, picks, and baskets; many of them, for the first few weeks, depending on borrowing from others. I have seen the written statement of the work of one man for sixteen days, which averaged 25 dollars per day; others have, with a shovel and pan, or wooden bowl, washed out 10 dollars to even 50 dollars in a day. There are now some men yet washing who have 500 dollars to 1,000 dollars. As they have to stand two feet deep in the river, they work but a few hours in the day, and not every day in the week.

A few men have been down in boats to this port, spending twenty to thirty ounces od gold, about 300 dollars. I am confident that this town (San Francisco) has one-half of its tenements empty, locked up with the furniture. The owners, store keepers, mechanics, and labourers--all gone to the Sacramento with their families. Small parties of five to fifteen men, have sent to this town and offered cooks ten to fifteen dollars per day for a few weeks. Mechanics and teamsters, earning the year past five to eight dollars per day, have struck and gone. Several U. S. volunteers have deserted. *U. S. Barque Anita*, belonging to the Army, now at anchor here, has but six men. One Sandwich Island vessel in port lost all her men; and was obliged to engage another crew at 50 dollars for the run of fifteen days to the Islands.

One American captain having his men shipped on this coast in such a manner that they could leave at any time, had them all on the eve of quitting, when he agreed to continue their pay and food; leaving one on board, he took a boat and carried them to the gold regions--furnishing tools and giving his men one-third. They have been gone a week. Common spades and shovels, one month ago worth 1 dollar, will now bring 10 dollars, at the gold regions. I am informed 50 dollars has been offered for one. Should this gold continue as represented, this town and others would be depopulated. Clerks' wages have risen from 600 dollars to 1,000 per annum, and board; cooks 25 dollars to 30 dollaars per month. This sum will not be any inducement a month longer, unless the fever and ague appears among the washers. *The Californian*, printed here, stopped this week. *The Star* newspaper office where the new laws of Governor Mason, for this country, are printing, has but one man left. A merchant, lately from China, has even lost his China servants. Should the excitement continue through the year, and the whale ships visit San Francisco, I think they will lose most of their crews. How Col. Mason can retain his men, unless he puts a force on the spot, I know not.

  I have seen several pounds of this gold, and consider it very pure and valuable in New York; 14 dollars to 16 dollars, in merchandise, is paid for it here. What good or bad effect this gold mania will have on California, I cannot fore tell. It may end this year; but I am informed that it will continue many years. Mechanics now in this town are only waiting to finish some rude machinery, to enable them to obtain the gold more expeditiously, and free from working in the river. Up to this time, but few Californians have gone to the mines, being afraid the Americans will soon have trouble among themselves, and cause disturbsnce to all around. I have seen some of the black sand, taken from the bottom of the river (It should in the States bring 25 to 30 cents per pound), containing many pieces of gold; they are from the size of the head of a pin to the weight of the eighth of an ounce. I have seen some weighing one-quarter of an ounce (4 dollars). Although my statements are almost incredible, I believe I am within the statements believed by everyone here. Ten days back, the excitement had not reached Monterey. I shall, within a few days, visit this gold mine, and will make another report to you.   In close you will have a specimen.

Joaquin Castro participated in comparatively few land sales. October 24, 1859, he sold one-third of his one-thirteenth share of the rancho to Charles Ford and Walker for $800. He participated in the collective sale to attorney Crane to finance legal fees with the rest of the heirs July 15, 1867. On October 30, 1869, he sold 160 acres of Rancho San Andrés to William A. Cornwall for $2,000. Together with Guadalupe and Simon he sold an interest in Rancho San Andrés to E. Tripp of San Francisco for $3,000. Joaquin was apportioned lots 43 and 59 in the 1873 partition; however, the sale of these in 1874 to Titus Hale apparently paid for his share of the damages.

Sometime in the later years Joaquin left Rancho San Andrés. We don't know precisely where he went after he left, or when specifically he departed after 1870. However, from books and articles about the bandit Tibutcio Vasquez we have an inkling of his whereabouts and his activities in the late sixties and seventies. These sources are often conflicting.

Tiburcio Vasquez, the Californio bandito was somewhat active in the Santa Cruz and Whiskey Hill (later called Freedom) areas. It has been said that Whiskey Hill is the spot where the residents of the Pajaro Valley went to quench their thirst and this does indeed seem to be the case. It sprang into existence at the juncture of the Santa Cruz Road (Freedom Boulevard) and the trail up to Green Valley (Green Valley Road) at about the same time that Watsonville began to grow on the banks of the Pajaro River. By 1852, it was already a motley collection of a dozen rude shanties scattered along the road, each one containing a cantina which catered to the vaqueros of the San Andrés and Los Corralitos Ranchos. They featured, not only whiskey but also gaming tables and hordes of randy women. The saloons and brothels of Whiskey Hill were said to be among the most wicked and wild in the state.

It was Jose Maria Gutierrez, who for many years ran the meanest little whorehouse at Whiskey Hill. The girls were hard, the gambling tables rigged, and the fandangos deadly. Gutierrez was a native of old Spain, who had arrived at California via Guadalajara, Mexico in 1845. A particularly exciting time at the Gurierrez saloon was on the 16th day of September during the celebration of Mexican Independence Day. This yearly fiesta was usually accompanied by at least one shooting or knifing. In 1872, the victim of a shooting was Garcia Rodriguez, a young bandido from Branciforte.

Another saloon and brothel which enjoyed a lively name at Whiskey Hill was operated by Jim Enemark. It ws here that Elsie Twitchell was working just prior to the day that she was stabbed by Benino Soqui during a quarrel under the Pajaro bridge. The incident almoat cost Elsie her life and resulted in Soqui spending eight years at San Quintin. After recuperation young Elsie returned to a life of sin at Enemark's.

Whiskey Hill's reputation for booze and lust spread far and wide making it a favorite watering hole for the likes of Joaquin Murrieta (so it is said), Tiburcio Vasquez, and Juan Soto, as well as local "bad boys" Faustino Lorenzana, Jose Rodriguez, and Ignacio Tejada. In 1877 the citizens decided to change the name of the village to Freedom perhaps in the hope that by adopting a more placid appellation there would be a corresponding change in reputation. If indeed that was a part of their thinking it proved to be singularly unsuccessful, as the fighting, drinking, and sinning continued on into the 20th century.

A professional gambler, Tiburcio would come around payday to the gambling dens frequented by the Miller and Luz vqueros such as the former Cracker Barrel in Whiskey Hill. Vasquez attempted to rob Henry Miller himself of his substantial payroll. He was famed for his bitterness against the Yankees starting as a youth of 15 in Monterey where he was suspected in the murder of Sheriff Hardmont. Considered a social bandit, he was supported and aided by the Californios who shared his rancor. One such was Joaquin Castro.

As early as 1867 Joaquin is said to have been at the New Idria Quicksilver Mines in Monterey County. We know from the Tiburcio Vasquez trial testimony of Joaquin Castro in 1875 that he was living on the Panoche in the Gavilans of south Monterey County in August 1874. He testified that Leiva (Vasquez' number one man) lived in Cantua Canyon and that he hired Joaquin to take his family south to San Emedio after an affair at Snyder's Store. They started on August 24, 1874, and arrived on August 28. Leiva was to pay Joaquin $300 for the job but instead gave him two mares, as related by the *San Jose Mercury*, July 14, 1875. Another source, *Beers*, reported that Leiva sent Joaquin Castro and his son to wait for him with his wife and horses at San Emedio where Joaquin received a share of the stolen property and then he and his son went north back to the New Idria Mine.

Joaquin was known as a compadre of Vasquez in a category with Greek George and others who furnished him aid. Jack Jones says that Vasquez and his men hid out at Joaquin's ranch when Cantua Canyon, his usual haunt got too hot. MacLean elsewhere says that Joaquin Castro was around the La Panza Mines (in southeast San Luis Obispo County) during godly excitement in the late 1870s and was considered a member of "The Vasquez Gang" at that time. MacLean characterizes these as men who may have developed only a little blindness where their fellow countrymen where concerned, yet may have crossed the line themselves. No record could be found in the Monterey County Recorder's Office of Joaquin Castro purchasing real estate in the 1860s or early 1870s.

Could bitterness over land dispossession prompt a scion of the respected Castro family of Watsonville to become involved with Vasquez? Perhaps, but Joaquin was undoubtedly upset about his oldest son Jose Pedro being lynched for presumed association with Vasquez in 1872. This could have prompted him to support Vasquez in the latters attempt to get away after the events at Snyder's Store in 1873, that resulted in Vasquez' hanging in San Jose in 1875.

After Joaquin Murieta, Tiburcio was probably the most notorious bandit California ever saw. He was born in Monterey in 1835. He attended school and could speak, read and write English. He committed his first known crime at age 14, stabbing a constable at a party. The circumstances of this crime are not altogether clear; it may have been accidental but whatever the true facts, Vasquez from this point on embarked on a life of crime. He joined a gang of desperados, and in time became the leader of his own group which ranged up and down central and southern California.

He was captured and convicted of horse-stealing and sent to San Quentin prison in 1857. He briefly escaped in 1859, was recaptured for again horse-stealing and was finally released after serving his full term in 1863.

In 1863, after committing a string of infamous robberies and murders in the San Benito area, Vasquez and some of his gang made their way to southern California. Over the course of several months, Vasquez managed to elude law enforcement officers by hiding in the canyons around the Tejon Pass. One of his favorite spots was the rock formation now known as Vasquez Rocks. After falling out with Vasquez one of the gang, Abdon Leiva, turned himself in to the authorities and agreed to turn States' evidence against Vasquez (it is believed that Leiva was motivated by jealously, as Vasquez had been having an affair with Leiva's wife Rosaria).

Still the bandit managed to elude authoritits for several months. He was finally captured in may of 1874 in the Arroyo Seco area of Los Angeles. He moved from Los Angeles to San Benito County, then to San Jose for trial. His jail cell became a major tourist draw. Thousands, most of them women, came to visit. Vasquez was charming to all, posing for photographs and giving out autographs. Convicted of two murders committed in Tres Pinos, he was sentenced to death. The only words he uttered from the gallows was, "Pronto."

After the 1870 census Jose Apolinario Castro, also known as Pedro, oldest son of Joaquin Castro, apparently moved to Monterey County in the vicinity of San Juan Bautista/Hollister where he operated a saloon. It seemed that he was married to, or lived with a relative of Vasquez, Concepcion Espinosa of the San Miguel Canyon/Prundale Espinosa family. This saloon was said to date back to about 1865 and was located near Pine Rock on property supposedly owned by Gonzales and Morano and was run by Joaquin's son Jose Castro. It was about 25 miles south of Hollister on the San Benito river. However, records in the Monterey County Recorder's Office indicate that Jose Castro actually purchased 160 acres in San Benito township on the east bank of the river on January 15, 1872, from Conception Vasquez. On the same date he purchaed all of her interest in a possessory claim to the Jose Castro Mining Company in San Benito. These transactions suggest that she may have gained a common law mariage interest in his mine and land. He also may have purchased the saloon itself from James McMahon in 1871.

According to the *Watsonville Pajaronian*, on Saturday, April 20, 1872, the San Benito Stage was robbed near Fred Taylor's store. The stage was stopped and the driver and passengers robbed of their money and valuables. The passengers were D. Upton Matthews, Mr. Billings, and a German. Several hundred dollars were taken. Tiburcio Vasquez was recognized as one of the robbers. Juan Jose Castro, keeper of the drinking shop on the road was suspected of complicity because the day before he went to Hollister with the same men and there saw them receive and handle considerable money. The following morning he was seen riding hard supposedly to prepare his comrades to rob the group, Jose Castro was arrested as an accomplice or principal, taken to the house of Edward J. Breen, and a Vigilante group took him in the night and hung him.

The *Monterey Democrat* published a few more details. Accordingly, Jose Castro was arrested and placed in custody by constable Willim McCool who placed him under guard at the Breem home. McCool went to get E. C. Tully, Esquire, as council for the defendant. In the night two masked men in a party of six or seven armed men, took Jose Castro by force, tied and blindfolded him and hung him from a nearby tree. Castro's age was estimated at 35 years and he died on the night of April 22, 1872. A coroner's inquest was held. J. W. Mathews was among the six men who signed the findings of the inquest. Warren Mathews of Bitterwater Valley kept a diary that revealed a few other details. He contends that Jose Castro was hung from a large willow tree 300 yards from the Breem house where they were guarding him. He was very heavy. The robbery took place where the bridge crosses the San Benito Creek a few miles above Paicines called "Robbers Roost" or Divigio's Crossing. One Dutch John was beset by bandits and Jose Castro was implicated in the stage coach robbery at Cornwell's.

The *Gilroy Democrat* published still more particulars. It stated that just below "Frank's Place," the stage was stopped by two Mexicans with masked faces and one carrying a Henry rifle and revolver (Vasquez had a Henry rifle). They ordered the driver to stop and get out. Mr. Billings and Dock Garner were ordered out, robbed and tied up. The robbers had already robbed Dutch John and tied him up by the side of the road. They went through all the trunks of Leonard & Billings, and the mail sack. They robbed a lad of $2 and then at the mouth of Williams Creek, they robbed Upton S. Mathews and Charles Pierce and tied them up too, then leaving for San Juan.

A Mr. Frank Alvarez reported that the lynching of Jose Castro took place near the Breen Brother's cattle corral about two miles from where the robbery occured. The paper condemned lynch law as it visits vengeance on innocent parties. None of these first hand accounts mentioned what possible role Jose castro had in the robberies other than being suspected of alerting the outlaws. The mystery was cleared up by Vasquez when he was in jail at San Jose awaiting trial for the Snyder Store murders at Tres Pinos. A reporter from the *San Jose Daily Patriot* iterviewed him in 1874 in his cell about the event in question, asking him if he and Juan Jose robbed the San Benito Stage. His response follows:

> No, Jose Castro was an innocent man. He was caught and hanged by the Vigilantes for the robbery, but he had nothing to do with it whatever. He is dead now, and I speak the truth and do justice to him. I was the man who planned and executed the robberies. I had one assistant, a young man, but I cannot give you his name. He kept a saloon on the San Benito, a short distance from the place where the stage was stopped, nothing more than this. His wife was Concepcion Espinos, who is a distant relation of mine. I used to happen into the saloon once in awhile; in fact I was there immediately preceding the robbery and I suppose that the people suspected Castro for these reasons. But not only was he innocent of taking an active part, but he knew nothing whatever about the matter beforehand.

One writer went so far as to say that Vasquez made his headquarters with Jose Castro in the San Benito District and he re-organized his band, resulting that one day Vasquez robbed the Hollister-benito Stage and several travelers. Another person writing after the fact, Dominga L. Cervantes Hoffer reported:

> It is said that Castro aided Vasquez by riding into Hollister, finding out if valuables would be in the express box, and what difficulties would

be encountered in holding up the stage. At first Castro was indirectly willing to help Vasquez, but not to take part in the actul crime. It was declared that Castro was compelled by Vazquez to join him and his gang in holding up the stage several miles from Castro's store.

Embroidering on the latter theme, Eugene T. Sawyer related:

> In the fall of 1871, while stopping at Castro's, the robbery of the San Benito Stage was planned. At first, Castro refused to take a hand. Vasquez taunted him with cowardice, when Castro drew a pistol, and the light of Tiburcio Vasquez would have then and there extinguished, had not the cap of the pistol snapped without igniting the powder. A hand-to-hand struggle followed and Castro was vanished. A reconciliation took place, and the saloon-keeper finally agreed to lend his assistance to the nefarious project. One other man, whose name Vasquez would not disclose, was also induced to join.

Francisco Floy Amador was born in Watsonville in 1864 and raised by his father Jose Maria Amador, son of Pedro Amdor. His father left fascinating recollections of early California taken by Thomas Savage, researcher of historian Hubert Howee Bancroft in 1877 when Amador was resident at Rancho San Andrés. Francisco attended school at Whiskey Hill until he was 14 and his father too old for work. Working for Miller and Luz as a woodcutter, Francisco eventually moved to Gilroy. His mother, Soledad Alviso Amador, was sister of Maria Antonia Amador, who was sister of Maria Amador, wife of Jose Joaquin Castro. Francisco referred to his Uncle Ignacio Castro as sometimes cleverly walking on his hands.

Francisco told of his brother Jacinto who was present at Snyder's store when the shooting occurred. Jacinto was told by one of Vasquez' men to lay down in a wagon and take cover. He reported that Vasquez came up later and followed his men after asking directions. Like Jacinto, Francicco Higuera was also in town and witnessed the shooting and told Francisco Amador the same story. No young teenagers present at the time came forward at the trial to testify as witnesses, but arrived later as he himself testified.

Francisco went on to explain that prior to the events at Snyder's Store in Paicines, Jose Castro and his wife and step-daughters had fed Vasquez' men at their nearby tavern which led to his being lynched. According to Francisco:

Jose's disappearance might have remained unsolved for some time except his dog "Calo" brought his master's hat home and the dog was induced to return to the place where it was immediately discovered that Jose had met with foul play and frofeited his life.

    The vigilantes took Jose to be a common person of the locality whereas Jose came of a prominent family from Santa Cruz, being one of the heirs of San Andrés Ranch, a holding of immense value for those days. Upon the step-daughters message back to the family homestead by wire, Jose's father brought the body of his son to the San Andrés Ranch near Watsonville, where he attended the wake and funeral of Jose. Through sources thus at hand, and later by way of conversations available, the nature of Jose's misfortune, and thus the background of the three murders at noon at Paicines in the 70s, was to form the basis for Tiburcio Casquez paying with his life.

The Death Index of Monterey County dated April 23, 1872, reports Jose Castro, white male, 35, occupation unknown, was hanged by a mob. None of this would be of immediate interest except for the fact that this Jose Castro was the oldest son of pioneer Joaquin Isidro Castro and who was the owner of Rancho San Andrés Castro Adobe, who once carved his initials and date upon its walls.

FOURTEEN

The grandest of all adobe buildings representing Northern California's rancho period is the two-story Cstro Adobe near Watsonville. This hacienda once featured a spacious fandango room on the second floor and an original one-story *cocina*, one of the only five such Mexican kitchens in the state. With its long, two-story proportions and full-width open balcony, it is a distinctly Monterey-Colonial building that demonstrates the expansion to the countryside of this celebrated architectural form from its original urban setting, at the end of the Mexican era (1821 - 1848).

Juan Jose Castro, a member of one of Alta Californias's most prominent founding families, built the large adobe house at historic Rancho San Andrés at around the time of the Gold Rush (between 1848 and 1849). His father, Jose Joaquin Castro, had come as a boy with his family to Northern California from Mexico with the pioneering Anza Expedition in 1775-76. Over time, the Castros were granted agricultural land from San Pablo Bay south to Monterey, as a reward for the family's military service and for their accomplishments as early settlers. By the 1840s, members of the Castro family ranched over a quarter of a million acres in Santa Cruz County alone. This adobe served as headquarter for the extended Castro family holdings; about 60 people, including Native American workers, lived in and around the building until 1883.

American-era lawsuits took a toll on Castro lands. Rancho San Andrés was originally two leagues in size, or about 11,000 acres, but was eroded over time through legal challenges and attorney's fees until the final partition of the rancho occurred in 1873. After partition, the adobe stayed in the hands of Juan Jose Castro, but its surrounding parcel had been reduced to just 40 acres. Apparently Juan Jose almost immediately lost title to this land as well, but he and his family stayed until 1883 when the Hansen family bought the property. The Hansens lived in the adobe until the 1906 Earthquake, after which they built a new house nearby on the property.

The adobe's next century embraces this and a succession of families who acted as stewards of this historic treasure. The historical significance of the 3,800 square-foot house was first recognized by owner Manuel E. Madiros in the mid 1930s, who urged the State to acquire it and had it reccorded by the Historic American Building Survey. The next owner, Frank Mello, saved it with a new roof according to local newspaper accounts. By then on June 20, 1940, Frank Mello Jr. received title to the Castro Adobe, retaining ownership through mid-1943, when he sold it and almost 40 acres to Alvin R. Holtzclaw. At this time the structure was vacant and in a rather run-down condition. George W. Holtzclaw purchased the Castro Adobe and 27.29 surroundibg acres in early 1945 from Alvin Holtzclaw, beginning a new stewardship of owners who lived in the Adobe. Over its long history the building has been the home of many multi-ethnic families and backdrop to a corresponding variety of events, from fandangos to jazz festivals.

In 1988, adobe conservationist Edna Kimbro and her husband, Joe, purchased the Castro Adobe from 20-year stewards, David and Elizabeth Potter. It was during the Kimbro's tenure that the 1989 Loma Prieta Earthquake severely damaged the house, but it was also during the Kimbro years when huge steps were taken to preserve the adobe for future generations. The restoration of the Castro Adobe was to be the fulfillment of Edna's and others' tireless efforts, personally and professionally, to bring the building back to its former glory.

Acquired by California State Parks in 2002, the Castro Adobe currently sits on one acre of land and contains a small orchard. An important and unusual aspect of the adobe is its rural location that retains much of the cultural landscape of the rancho era, and the original *carreta* path---Old Adobe Road. The authentic early California building and its setting possess tremendous potential for interpretation of the rural lifestyle and culture of Mexican California for the benefit of present-day residents of Pajaro Valley, Santa Cruz County, and the Central Coast region. The ultimate potential of the Castro Adobe at Rancho San Andrés can now be realized, since its stabilization and restoration have been completed. The Friends of Santa Cruz County State Parks and the Community Foundatin of Sant Cruz County have been greatly gratified since this vision of restoration is now a reality.

The Castro Adobe, includng the 1-acre parcel, is the last remnant of the Casto family's land holdings in the Rancho San Andrés, one of seven land holdings in Santa Cruz County that at their peak totaled over 250,000 acres. The Castro family originally came to California with the Anza Colonizing Expedition of 1775-1776 that claimed much of Northern California for Spain. Subsequently, the Castros became the largest Californio (original Spanish and Mexican) family in Alta California, with rancho land grants throughout the Central Coast, ranging from San Pablo Bay to Monterey.

A two-story, approximately 4,000 square foot adobe was built circa 1849 on what is now Old Adobe Road as the headquarters for the Castro family, with nearly 60 people living in and around the property. It is significant as the only full two-story adobe rancho building ever constructed in the Monterey Bay region and is the largest rural hacienda in the region. It complements the urban adobe dwellings in Monterey and San Juan Bautista and is the oldest structure and only State landmark in the Pajaro Valley.

It is interesting to note the date of construction, name of the builder, and a few other details of the Rancho San Andrés Castro Adobe have varied somewhat within some of the quoations presented above, essentially due to the various writers having sought their research from different sources, some of which were not reliable at the time. Depending upon which paper the reporters may have read or whom they may have talked to, they have been presented with different conclusions.

For example, it is held by some writers that Jose Joaquin Castro was the sole builder of the Castro Adobe and by other writers that it was built by his son Juan Jose Castro. Also, indications of dates of its construction have varied widely. But since these declarations, new research has evolved; it is now known that Jose Joaquin Castro did not construct the Castro Adobe completely by himself. New investigations have shown that it was finished circa 1849, and he died in 1838.

Historians now believe that Jose Joaquin Castro built the first part of the Rancho San Adrés Castro Adobe, a one story structure with an adjoining kitchen on the north side. In some articles Jose is often referred to as Joaquin, his midddle name and his father's first name, the two of which are not to be confused during the era of adobe construction. His father died in 1803, many years even before construction began on the Castro Adobe.

Jose Joaquin Castro died in 1838, perhaps after he had finished the first story structure and lived in it awhile, leaving the hacienda to his son Jose Joaquin Castro, who is believed to have enlarged the family home to a two-story showplace. The date of construction is believed by historians to be circa 1849, an eara within the lifespan of Juan Jose Castro. Consequently, based now on new evidence, both Jose Joaquin Castro and Juan Jose Castro are both deemed its builder; neither one was singularly the primary builder, even though we often see the adobe stated as being the Joaquin Castro Adobe, inferring it to have been solely built and owned by Joaquin (Jose), even though Juan Castro's effort was possibly as great or greater in the construction, and who also owned the adobe for years.

As happened to most of the land owning Californio families, the Castro family's land holdings were disolved in the decades following California's annexation to the United States. The adobe passed into non-Castro family ownership in the late 19th century and continued to serve as a family residence, with relatively modest modifications, up until the Loma Prieta earthquake of 1989. One of the more noteworthy additions is an inner walled garden on the west side of the adobe in the 1960s designed by Thomas Church, the renowned landscape architect. The surrounding grounds also contain the remnants of an old orchard, although many of the trees are believed to not be part of the original landscaping design.

The Loma Prieta earthquake of 1989, measured a magnitude 6.9, caused significant structural damage to the Castro Adobe, including the collapse of its south wall that rendered it unsafe for residential or other occupancy. Up until then, there was no major damage suffered by the Castro Adobe, even since the San Francisco earthquake of larger estimated magnitude of 7.7 to 8.5. It is believed though that throughout the years there had been an accumulation of damage to the adobe walls of the Castro Adobe from numerous earthquakes throughout the years of its existence. Because of earthquakes, it had added minor cracks in its walls here and there since it was built, stressing it to an ultimate unstable limit, but up to the time of the Loma Prieta earthquake there was no apparent major damage.

Since 1855, soon after the Castro Adobe was built, 40 earthquakes of magnitudes greater than 5.5 have occured on the San Andreas Fault system in coastal California, up until the current time. Perhaps the break down of the adobe's walls by these numerous, smaller earthquakes over the interval prior to and since the San Francisco earthquake is reason for the extreme damage from the Loma Prieta eathquake, of less magnitude than the San Francisco earthquake.

Since that time the building was closed and somewhat stabilized and protected from weather, up and until renovation was begun and finally completed. During this time, numerous individuals and organizations worked to devise a solution that would restore the historically significant Castro Adobe and ensure its long-term preservation. Through the efforts of Assemblyman Fred Keeley, legislation was finally passed in 1999 to fund acquisition and rehabilitation to add the Castro Adobe to the California State Park System, in recognition of its historic significance and the opportunity it represents to interpret early California history, particularly for the large numbers of Mexican and other Latino residents of the Pajaro Valley area.

The addition of the historic Castro Adobe to the California State Paark System presents an opportunity to preserve one of the oldest and most historically significant structures in Santa Cruz County. However, at the insistence of the Governor's office, the legislation that authorized adding the Castro Adobe to the State Park System also contained a requirement that the costs for the future management and operation of the Castro Adobe be funded from non-State sorces. This is different than the typical operation of State Park units, which are taxpayer funded through appropriations from the Legislature. This created a significant challenge because revenue generating uses or obtaining other sources of revenue must occur in a manner that is appropriate to the historic semi-rural setting and does not detract from the State Park's ability to host the public, school groups, and others at the adobe for interpretive and other programs.   Prior to any restoration on the Castro Adobe, Bay Area Econonics (BAE), a national real estate economics and development consulting firm with extensive experience in park facilities and historic preservation, was retained by the County of Santa Cruz to prepare a reuse feasibility study focused on appropiate uses and management arrangements to achieve self-sufficiency. BAE worked with the ad hoc committee for the Castro Adobe and a smaller Steering Committee to review uses, management options, and other issues. The study was quite estensive.

    The study found that due to the Castro Adobe's relatively remote location, its small building and site size, and the limited area for parking, there are significant physical and market constraints on the types of uses that are both feasible and able to generate sufficient revenues. The County's Agricultural zoning of the site limits commercial uses. The one-lane private access road, Old Adobe Road, does not meet County standards for access to commercial uses. At the same time, State Parks' exemption from local zoning regulations and responsibilty for planning, public safety and code enforcement provides critical flexibility in creating an appropriate State Park with revenue generating uses. State Park will need to work closely with the Old Adobe Road neighbors to promote a harmonious relationship.

    Based on a review of many potential uses for the Castro Adobe, and the need to ensure sufficient revenues for management and operating costs, BAE believed that the most appropriate revenue generating use is meetings and special events, including family and social events and fee programs. This use would be compatible with the school field trips, interpretive and cultural programs, and other public programs and visitation typical of State Park units. Based on an estimated annual operating budget of approximately $52,000, the number necessary annual revenue generating events is approximately 46 on weekend days and holidays and 17 on weekdays. Daily use fees are projected to range from $600 to $900 per day based upon analysis of comparable facilities.

    State Parks and the Friends of Santa Cruz State Parks, an independent non-profit supporting the State Parks in Santa Cruz County, agreed that the Friends would be responsible for the future management and operation of the Castro Adobe. Because of the park focus of this organization and its agreement with State Parks, it may be able to operate the Castro Adobe with fewer revenue events.

In State Fiscal Year 2001-2002, working construction drawings and bid documents were prepared for the rehabilitation of the Castro Adobe, including future identified repairs or improvements to Old Adobe Road. The state also sought to secure a contractor for the work at this time. Construction was projected to commence in approximately July, 2002, but did not get into high gear until sometime after that date. As of the date of this writing the Castro Adobe has been completely rehabilitated and earthquake proofed and there has been much jubilation about its successful completion.

Initially, prior to beginning of rehabilitation of the Rancho San Andrés Castro Adobe, Friends of Santa Cruz State Parks began their volunteer work on a rather mass scale. "One brick at a time" was their motto, and it certainly was the process for saving the adobe as volunteers endured heavy lifting, wheelbarrowing, dirt sifting, and punching mud into wood molds to hand make the vital adobe bricks needed in the future re-construction of the adobe's deteriated walls. The dedicated members of Friends of Santa Cruz State Parks, and the Friend's staff and board have done an excellent job in facilitating the means for initial rehabititation of the Castro Adobe, as well as staying on the job throughout its finalization in 2009, a time when they could lift their heads high with pride. They are all to be highley commended for such great work and dedication.

But perhaps such a successful climax would never have happened had it not been for the persistant effort of Edna Kimbro's diligent encouragement, and her strong drive to rehabilitate her beloved Rancho San Andrés Castro Adobe. Friends of Santa Cruz State Parks, soon after her death on August 6, 2003, prsented a composite of the many achievements of this eliquent lady who tirelessly advocated for the preservation of the California adobes, four of which were located in Santa Cruz County, and including the Castro Adobe. The connotation given below stands as a memorial to her and her achievements and is an appros quote to be introduced at this juncture of this writing:

Edna Kimbro, born on June 25, was raised in Monterey and San Jose. She graduated from Monterey High School and it was in Monterey where she aquired her love of early California architecture.

For several years she lived with her mother and Aunt Zukie just outside of the walls of the Mission San Carlos Borromeo in Carmel where her acute appreciation of the decorative arts was applied in their antique store.

In 1969, she married Joe Kimbro, whom she shared a love of blue grass music, wine, and the arts. The couple moved to Santa Cruz in 1972 where Edna was enrolled at University of California at Santa Cruz, studying history with an emphasis on the decorative arts.

Her senior thesis topic was the Herter Brothers, a firm of the 19th century architects and furnature designers who had prominent families such as the Hopkins and the Vanderbilts as clients. Her well researched thesis was the basis of a book and exhibit on the Herter Brothers at the Metropolitan Museum of Art in New York.

In 1975, the Kinbros prchased the Branciforte Adobe, the last surviving adobe associated with the Villa de Branciforte. During their restoration of the adobe Edna did extensive research into its history.

She was the life force and co-founder in 1981 of the Adobe Coalition, a group of advocates that facilitated the restoration of the Santa Cruz Mission Adobe building on School Street in Santa Cruz to its pre-secularization period. Edna led political and community awareness and fund raising campaigns to secure a sound and historically accurate future for the Mission Adobe as a California State Paark.

Following the success of the Mission Adobe campaign, Edna was contracted as the principal research historian for the California Department of Parks and Recreatiion Archeological and Investigations, and developed the furnishings plan for portions of the Mission Adobe's interior.

During the 1980s Edna was a consulting historian for State Parks working primarily in Santa Cruz, Monterey and Ventura counties. Her work with primary documents of the pre-statehood period resolved previously misunderstood community and land ownership roles for post-mission Native Americans in Santa Cruz, much of which is interpreted now at the Santa Cruz Adobe.

She served on the board of the Caliornia Mission Studies Association in San Juan Capistrano and contributed heavily to scholary interpretation of the state's mission era. During this period she conducted a self-directed intensive study of the art of the missions, locating and identifying many of the extant paintings that had been widely scattered following the mission secularization.

In 1989, the Kimbros purchased the Rancho San Andrés Castro Adobe in the Pajaro Valley with the intent to preserve, restore and live in it. That same year Edna was one of two persons from the United States to attend the International Centre for the Study of the Preservation and Restoration of Cultural Property Programm in Rome. For six months she studied issues related to the conservation of reinforced masonry buldings, conservation of earthen structures, and preservation treatment of designated historic communities.

Soon after her return, the Kimbro's beautiful Castro Adobe was severely danaged by the Loma Prieta Earthquake. A FEMA trailer became the Kimbro's primary residence for five years while a new home was built on adjacent land, where Edna and Joe could keep a close watch on the crumbling adobe nearby.

In 1990, thanks to Edna and others, the Castro Adobe was designated a State Historic Landmark. Edna's continuing campaign to save the adobe resulted in its purchase and designation as a California State Historic Park.

During the 1990s, Edna continued her consulting focusing on California's adobes, including several of the California Missions, the Santa Barbara Presidio, and the Monterey Presidio Chapel, along with Rancho Camulos, the Southern California site of the early novel Ramona.

She co-authored a successful National Historic Landmark Application for Santa Ines Mission which is still used as a model by National Parks service staff. In 1999, she co-authored a book on seismic retrofitting of California's historic adobe buildings sponsored by the Getty Conservation Institute. In recent years, Edna was a California State Park Historian, based in Monterey, where she worked on the documentation of the many adobe buildings in the State park system. It was always her dream that the Rancho San Andrés Castro Adobe would become a State park.

With the support of the Friends of the Castro Adobe and State Assemblyman Fred Keeley, this dream was realized in 2001 with work beginning that summer to retrofit the fragile adobe.

In 2003, Edna was awarded the California Mission Studiies Association's Noran Neuerburg Award in recognition of her role as advocate for the preservation and interpretation of California's mission past.

On August 6th, more than two hundred friends, family and colleagues from around the world gathered at the Santa Cruz Historic Park to share their respect, honor and love of Edna Kinbro, after her demise.

Their lives have been enriched by her passionate pursuit to preserve mission period art and California's historical adobes.

Friends of Santa Cruz State Parks worked hard to help fund the full restoration of the Rancho San Andrés Castro Adobe, once home to the late respected Edna Kimbro. This extremely rare mid-1800s, two-story Monterey style adobe and historic grounds is now a State Park, thanks to the work of Edna Kinbro, former assembly member Fred Keeley, and other ardent preservationists determined to protect the irreplaceable beauty of this rare home grounds, and to preserve and share its priceless California heritage.

Now fully restored, the Castro Adobe embodys the post-mission California, pre-American period of history here on the central coast, when California was Alta Mexico. One of the few remaining original adobes in the state of California, this building is an outstanding example of the fine, adobe building done in our region in the 1800s.

The 1989 Loma Prieta earthquake damaged the Castro Adobe to such an extent that it needed careful seismic retrofit repair. Recent research and technology offered new and safer ways of supporting, protecting and extending the life of historic adobe structures. This new technology has helped to preserve the Castro Adobe for many years to come.

Suzanne Paizis, activist and former Castro Adobe owner did much in promoting the preservaation of the Castro Adobe with her writing, encourgement, and personal ambassadorship for the adobe's survival. Now deceased, she is greatly missed by all, memorialized by many, as brought out below in a recent tribute to her:

Born in Chicago on July 6, 1924, she attended public schools and graduated from Senn High School in 1942. She studied ballet and toured with a dance company on the East Coast. After a brief interlude of living and working on a farm in Michigan, she moved with her family to Monterey in 1949, where her brother was stationed at Fort Ord. She earned an associate's degree from Monterey Penninsula college in 1952, and briefly attended San Francisco State, where she met her husband, John Paizis. They lived in Carmel Valley until 1959, then bought the historic Castro Adobe near Watsonville, where they lived until 1963.

Soon after moving to Santa Cruz area, Mrs. Paizis joined the Unitarian Universalist Fellowship, where she helped start a successful Sunday school program. She earned a bachelor's degree and teaching credential from San Jose State in 1966 and became a teacher and reading specialist for the Freedom and Live Oak School districts. In 1967, she helped found the Santa Cruz chapter of Lyceum, a program for gifted children, and became its first president.

Mrs. Paizis served as president of the Cabrillo Music Festival from 1963 to 1965 and was one of the members of the music festival's inaugural board. She was a board member of the League of Women Voters and helped organize the local Chapter of the National Organization for Women in 1971. Hoping to be the first woman elected to the state Senate, she ran for that office in 1972 and was unopposed for the Democratic nomination, believing representation by qualified women would lead to new approaches to solving problems. Her bid was unsuccessful, but she inspired other women to seek political office.

Mrs. Paizis decided to run against the 26-year-incumbent state Senator Donald Grunsky after meeting with him about school financing. She said, "His attitude toward us was like we were a bunch of little housewives who shouldn't be worringing about such complicated matters," the *Sentinel* reported at the time. Some other aspects of her platform were that the government needed to become more relevant and accountable to the people.

Mrs. Paizis also wanted women to become more active in local, state and national poliitics to bring more balance to the government. After her campaign, she wrote, *Getting Her Elected--The Political Woman's Handbook,* a manual designed to help organize their own campaigns. She was a founding member of the Santa Cruz County Women's Commission, and served as executive director between 1975 and 1978. During her tenure, the Women's Crisis Support program and Women's Shelter were established. She also helped coordinate the Santa Cruz County Council for gifted children.

She enjoyed gardening, family history, consuming the chocolate dessert concoctions of her son-in-law, Jason Cronin, and she delighted in her grandchildren, Nicole Cronin, and Franklin Jones. She enthusiastically shared her intellectual curiosity and historically informed opinions with others. Most recently, she spent her time reading and researching Shakespeare's true identity.

In recent years she belonged to the Santa Cruz Genealogical Society, and worked as a volunteer for the Santa Cruz Sentinel Indexing Project. In 2002, she published *The Joaquin Castro Adobe in the Twentieth Century--From Earthquake to Earthquake,* a book chronicling the history of the Castro Adobe from the 1906 earthdquake to the Loma Prieta earthqake in 1989. Like her friend Edna Kimbro, she too looked forward with zest to the renovation of the Castro Adobe. Their dreams have now been finalized.

Proof

Made in the USA
Charleston, SC
10 February 2010